How to Start
Silk Screening
on a Shoestring
and Make Up to
$1,000,000

by

Paul McDonald

Paul's Bookshelf Publications
P.O. Box 655
Pottsville, Arkansas 72858
(501) 967-5132

Dedicated to my wife, Bobbeye Shirl who I know loves me very much and who I know I need and depend on very much.

Paul's Bookshelf Publications
Pottsville, Arkansas 72858
501-967-5132

ISBN 1 - 89058 - 00 - 9

TABLE OF CONTENTS

INTRODUCTION

SHORT HISTORY OF SCREENPRINTING

Wearing a printed T-shirt is perhaps the fastest way to get a message across to anyone who cares to look. But the message can change quickly . . . like tomorrow. Screenprinting has evolved into a unique industry due to its unlimited growth and easier accessibility to printing equipment.

As far as modern technology is concerned, the first T-shirt screenprinting machine arrived on the scene in the mid 1950's. Initially, the T-shirt was primarily sold as a souvenir. As people journeyed on vacations, the imprinted beach towels also became popular.

By the 1960's larger and faster equipment was developed. As the mood of the country changed, T-shirts slowly became the way for anyone to make a statement, simply by putting his message on a T-shirt and be seen.

Within twenty years or so, screenprinting beat to a different drum and is no longer considered just a fad. More sophisticated equipment became available as our economy also expanded. Screenprinting has become very diverse and the equipment has speeded up production. Now computers have entered the field to help keep track of hundreds of options and compile thousands of bits of information.

As production increases, the marketplace will also open up new avenues for the industry to expand. Although the T-shirt has been the center of growth, there are endless items that screenprinters work with. There are caps, of course. Or think about towels, mousepads, license plates, signs, posters, banners, jackets, neckties, mugs, umbrellas, aprons, bags or most anything else you can think about printing on. All these I have done with a minimum of effort, with the simplest of equipment and small investment.

Today there are thousands of sophisticated transfers that are available to the screenprinter. The small printer now can order in minimum quantities. He or she can apply the transfer to a T-shirt with a shirt heat press. This can double or triple the value of a five-dollar T-shirt. Or place a transfer onto a cap with a cap press and easily double your investment. But then, you will not be paying five dollars for a T-shirt or even two dollars for a cap. Literally, I will help you buy them wholesale.

T-shirt, cap and other types of merchandise vendors can be found at most any kind of event, whether it be sporting, social, festival or simply business. Promoters realize that there is a market for various group merchandising. They need screenprinters since they are constantly on the threshold of new and repetitive events. They need a T-shirt for advertising purposes plus serve as a souvenir for the participants. Every marathon runner wants his/her neighborhood to know that he/she participated in the event. The promoter needs the entry fee for fund-raising purposes. The participants want a souvenir for this investment. You cannot visit a shopping mall without seeing evidence of a rock concert that took place or some sporting event about to take place.

Welcome to an exciting as well as crazy industry. You can become part of it with a small or a large investment. You can start small and create your own personal gifts for friends and family. Or from a small beginning allow yourself to progress into a multimillion dollar business. This book is primarily for the newcomer who has little or no experience with screenprinting. It will introduce simple manual equipment - some of which can be easily made by the "do-it-yourself" minded individual. It will likewise introduce the novice to available equipment for the serious-minded individual who is in a hurry to get started.

This book will provide a great deal of information: names, addresses and phone numbers of many firms who will eagerly supply catalogs and pricing of their merchandise. Most will have 1–800 numbers so you do not even have to sit down and mail out inquiries.

There will be some information about the tax permit that will be required for you before ordering and receiving merchandise at wholesale pricing. You will be able to purchase Hanes, Fruit–of–the–Loom, Jerzees and other nationally known brands - even at prices less than a sale at Walmart.

Silk screening has become a crazy business that has limitless opportunities and much flexibility. You may start as a fledgling printer and later branch into embroidery. You may work to produce your own business or expand into wholesaling for others. You can explore both markets . . . custom work for your own clients or do contract work for others.

You can live in the country and operate your own shop . . . at home. And yet have most of your customers call you some 25 to 100 miles away. Some of my shirts are in Canada and as far away as Italy. How about that?

The T-shirt entrepreneur does not have a mandatory retirement age. (I started after I retired.) Nor is there a minimum starting age. Gifted or motivated high school students have started this business from scratch . . . long on incentive but short on investment capital. Others got their families involved as part-time help whenever large jobs came in or deadlines had to be met.

In a recent national screenprinter magazine, a national survey pointed out just how quickly one can rise and expand in this industry. One silk screen printer (founded in 1994) had over one million imprints with ten employees within one year. Another company reported over a million pieces printed and it was only five years old. Still another, nearly five million pieces and yet under ten years in business. But the vast majority of screen printshops have five employees or less and remain a family business.

Our best advice to you as you get started:
1. Do not try to grow too fast. Grow, but under control. Know as you grow, you will have to recruit and train good help.
2. Always strive to accept jobs that you can handle.
3. And when you accept a job, try your best to meet the deadlines you set. Your customers will remember your deadlines that you set.
4. Never get into bidding wars with other printers. Always remember there is NO reason to work for NO PROFIT. You cannot remain in business long without profit.

5. Commit your business to both SERVICE and QUALITY. When and if you do both, you will prosper.

6. And finally remember . . . SERVICE . . . SERVICE . . . SERVICE.

Chapter 1

THE SCREEN

The screen-making process is the most important aspect of silk screening. A good or bad job hangs in the balance. It all begins with the screen itself. Simply stated, the screen is a mesh fabric stretched over a frame on which a stencil has been attached. The artwork for the stencil will be taken up separately. First, let us talk about the fabric.

THE FABRIC

The screen printing mesh holds your stencil in place and allows the ink to pass through onto the substrate (e.g., whatever is being printed like a T–shirt, jacket, bag or whatever.) There are several different mesh types that include silk, multifilament polyester and monofilament polyester.

We mention silk since it was the first most widely used mesh material (therefore the term silk screening.) However, it is seldom used today. And so for our purposes, silk has become "a thing of the past."

MULTIFILAMENT MESH

Multifilament mesh is a polyester, synthetic fiber made up of multifilament threads (woven threads) twisted to form a single yarn or thread. The letter 'X, is shown after a

1

number to denote the quality fineness of its weave. In silk screening, the double 'XX, quality would range between 6XX and 25XX. The higher the number would mean there would be smaller mesh openings for the ink to travel through.

MONOFILAMENT

MULTIFILAMENT

MONOFILAMENT MESH

For us, the choice is easy. Monofilament mesh is a high quality polyester fabric. Monofilament is a single smooth round fiber woven into a weaving mesh. It can accept high tension on your screen frames with little trouble. The smooth surface provides a fine quality for printing plus easy follow-up cleaning. Monofilament meshes are denoted by the actual number of threads in inches. In most everyday usage, the main meshes range between 60 and 360 threads per inch. Monofilament mesh requires direct emulsion only. Monofilament fabrics have very good abrasion resistance, high stability and a regular mesh structure, all of which are required for fine quality printing.

Comparison chart between multifilament and

Monofilament polyester fabrics

Multifilament	Monofilament
6XX	86
8XX	139
10XX	160
12XX	200
14XX	225
16XX	245
18XX	260
20XX	280
25XX	300

Rule of thumb for proper selection might be:

1. For printing shirts, jackets - 8 xx to 10 xx - 160 mesh

2. For most other surfaces 12 xx to 16 xx 200 to 260 mesh.

MESH COLOR

There are several dyed color meshes available. They are dyed at the factory. The colors come chiefly in yellow and orange. But there are other colors. Be aware that colored meshes require longer exposure time. It also should be noted that they may hold detail better than white (undyed) mesh.

The chief purpose of color fabrics is to filter ultraviolet light during the screen exposure. The theory being that light might pass through white fabrics and expose unwanted areas to the light. But for us beginners, white is fine.

The open area of a screen is that position of the screen surface that the ink passes through. Of course, the rest of the area is the mesh portion of the screen. The mesh opening should be three times greater than the ink pigment size. This will be especially important should fluorescent and/or metallic inks be used.

MESH COUNT
The mesh count here in the United States is usually stated as threads per inch (TPI.) So when you see 110TPI (or simply 110) you will know the mesh has 110 threads per inch.

The mesh opening is the distance across the space between two parallel threads. This distance is usually expressed in microns (unit of measurement that is a millionth of a meter.) The diameter of the mesh thread is also measured in microns. You can analyze the mesh fabric with a mesh counter that can determine what the actual count of a fabric is. You can secure a mesh counter from your dealer supplier. (Note: Dealers and suppliers are all listed in the appendix of this book.) I have never had one since I mark my screens when I receive them from my regular supplier. But as fabrics accumulate, it may become increasingly more difficult to distinguish between many fabrics. This would become important as you need to select the proper fabric for a given job. The mesh counter is a simple device placed on the screen and rotated until a 'star, points to the correct count. A pocket magnifier can also give you the thread counts and becomes a useful tool for film inspection, half tones, and other printing checks. Many small shops do not have a mesh counter, relying instead on hand feel or mesh marks made on the screen or simply coded on the screens when received.

Until recently, 110 mesh monofilament was considered the most common screen fabric for textile screen printers. But with improved technology, new ink formulas have been developed. These improved inks have led to a creamier texture that has become easier to print and work with. They are also easier to clean and reclaim. According to a recent publication these constant improvements have prompted many screen printers to raise their screen mesh to and average of 127. I still use 110 for textile printing and 160 for nylon jackets. Your supplier representative can help you in your choice based on the jobs you have under consideration. Once the frame has been selected, you will next decide the type of mesh to use, which means the correct count for the print job you are getting ready to print.

For textile printing, I repeat that monofilament polyester will provide your sharpest print and exercise the tightest control over your ink deposit.

Simply remember that the higher mesh counts (with many small openings) will identify your finer textured fabrics. And the lower mesh counts (with large openings) will identify coarser fabrics. So match your mesh counts to your type of printing.

SUGGESTED MESH COUNT FOR THE TYPE OF INK OR PRINTING

20-40	Glitter inks with large glitter particles
60-85	Glitter and Puff ink
85-110	Heavy, high opacity inks such as white printing applications such as athletic numbers and dark fabrics
110-170	Most plastisol inks for general printing Most of your printing will be in this range
175-230	Fine detail printing
230-260	Process printing on manual equiment

TENSIONED SCREENS

When you prepare your own screens, you realize quickly that correctly tensioned screens are vital to the quality of your printed work. You may wish to purchase a tension meter to help you achieve proper tensioned screens, whether your screens were purchased from a supplier or were made in–house by yourself. Most applications in a manual screenprinting shop should average between 22 and 30 newtons (newton is a unit of measurement used in screen fabric tensioning and expressed as newtons per centimeter) and be taut enough to produce good quality prints. Your mesh supplier will be happy to furnish you with a copy of their recommended mesh tension levels.

In time you will become aware that there may be significant differences between the same counts of different brands. So using the same brand should mean that the mesh characteristics such as thread diameter, tension strength and mesh opening size should all remain the same. Therefore it would be advisable to locate a reputable supplier you are comfortable with, one who supplies a quality and consistent product and stay with that firm. Most suppliers have technicians who are happy to furnish knowledgeable troubleshooting help whenever you need it. This is especially true when you purchase regularly from that firm. And finally a word of caution. If you start with wood frames stretched to 20 newtons and they are giving you the good results you seek, there would be no reason to change frames although current literature may frequently suggest that you should update your frames.

PRETREATMENT

Normally when you purchase mesh fabrics, be aware that the fabric must undergo a pretreatment process to remove any oil or dust that may have been caused by handling. Pretreatment will insure better stencil adhesion. Without pretreatment the mesh may suffer from pin holes, have poorer quality images of your work and may not even produce a usable screen.

DEGREASER AND CLEANING SCREENS

Some industrial cleaners and degreasers can be used but the use of general household detergents is frowned upon by the experts. However, I have always washed my new screens with a mild dishwashing liquid in warm water. I have had good results over the years. After this hand washing and rinsing, I simply iron the screen dry (with wife's iron of course). The screen is then made smooth and will receive the emulsion easily.

Degreasing is also a simple procedure. Brush on a degreaser, let stand two or three minutes and then rinse with cold water. Since your screen is a polyester fabric (and provided you have no regular degreaser) you may substitute a 10% caustic soda solution to both sides of the screen. Follow this procedure with a cold water rinse.

Proper cleansing (pretreatment) of the screen will reduce 'pin holes, caused by dust particles and 'fish eyes, caused by any oil or grease left on the screen. If the screen were not properly pretreated, these 'pin holes, and 'fish eyes, would have to be 'blocked out, after the screen is exposed.

BLOCKOUT

Blockout is a chemical liquid applied to cover any pin holes or other imperfections in the screen. Once the liquid dries on the screen ink cannot leak onto the garments being printed.

Applying blockout to the screen is an easy task. You hold the screen up against a bright light to locate any pin holes or other imperfections in the screen. You dip a cotton swab or pointer pen into the liquid blockout and fill all these holes. You do not want any ink to ruin your garments so even the most minute holes need to be filled. You apply the blockout to the back side of the screen. Once you have completely covered all the holes, you allow the blockout to dry on the screen. Once dried, it does not hurt to check the screen against the light to be sure all holes are covered.

A clean screen means there should be better coatability of the liquid emulsion. Clean screens also ensure against premature screen breakdown and fewer pin holes to block out.

ABRASION

Abrasion can also become a part of the screen preparation whenever the stencil does not adhere properly to the smooth surface of the screen mesh. Abrading the screen simply means scratching the surface of the screen to allow the stencil process to cling better to the screen. Most often this will pertain to indirect emulsion and capillary film. This is something you should know about even though it may not be required very often when working with the direct emulsion process. The abrasion process is accomplished by applying a silicon carbide or an aluminum oxide powder to a wet screen. Work it in by circular motion with a polyester or nylon brush. Only a few second's wait is required and then rinse.

The abrasion process is followed by degreasing and the routine steps of pretreatment.

FABRIC SIZES

All fabric meshes are sold by the yard and they usually come in stock widths of 42", 52", 66", and 72". Consider the frames you plan to cover and it will help you decide the best width size. Strive to avoid as much waste as you can. Small leftover scraps after framing are lost profits that cannot be reclaimed. Once you figure out how you plan to divide the screens, cut them into more manageable sizes. You will need to pretreat each before use.

Chapter 2

THE FRAMES

There are three basic types of screen frames that are readily available. They are wood, metal, and retensionable.

Wood has been the most common frame used in the small manual screen printing shop. They work very well for most printing jobs. Wood frames when purchased commercially should be made of kiln-dried wood that usually have mortise-and-tenon corners for strength. A protective polyurethane coating is highly desirable to protect against moisture during washout and reclaiming. If you make your own frames, be sure the sides are sanded smooth and there are no splinters that might damage your screen fabric. Splinters also play havoc with your hands.

Corrugated Fasteners

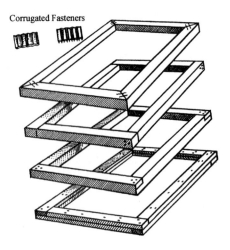

1. Most common and easiest to make.

2. Square joints using wood screws.

3. Make the end half lap joint.

4. Use double pieces and get half lap effect.

WOODEN FRAMES

Many new screen printers are in a hurry to get started and will frequently order a small number of pre–assembled frames. In this way they can more easily see how they are put together and help them judge whether they wish to make their own frames. Two 19" x 22" frames with 110 mesh came with my 4–color printer. I made my other 50 to 60 frames until I ordered my first retensionable screens some four to five years ago. But I continue to make smaller screens as required.

Remember that you can print quality work using wood frames. The wood frame should be heavy enough to prevent twisting — especially after extended use and numerous reclaiming operations.

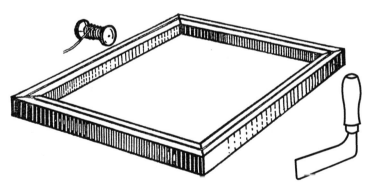

The Grooved Frame
The screen is attached by forcing a waxed cord into the groove using a stretch tool.

STRETCHING DEVICES

There are a number of stretching devices that can help you to achieve tension on your home made screens.

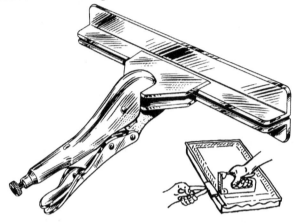

Note this sturdy all–metal pliers equipped with a pair of sure grip rubber strips ten inches long. (Rubber strips which prevent the mesh fabric from slipping.) With rubber strips locked onto the mesh, stretching is made easy by applying pressure against the edge of the frame. If your wood frame is grooved for receiving the stretch cord, then use the 5–inch stretch tool designed to push the cord into the grooved area. Work your way around the screen with your stretcher and the stretched tool. Release the pressure of the grip jaws by flipping the lever of the pliers.

If you make your own frames, you can make the grooved area with your table saw. Make sure you do not make the grooved area too wide or too deep.

The 5–inch cord stretching tool is available from your supply dealer. The stretch cord (also from your supply dealer) is made of polyethylene designed to expand in the grooved frame. However, it is easy to remove and will allow the frame to be re-stretched again in the future.

Many a wood frame has received staples applied with a regular staple gun tacker. (Reg 1/4" staples can be purchased from local hardware store.) The compression spring action of the staple gun will staple the stretched fabric to the wood frame. Make sure all staples are snug against the fabric to prevent the fabric from tearing.

You may also use some nylon staple tape to keep the fabric from ripping, slipping, or acquiring damage from using staples. You simply tape under or over the mesh and staple onto the frame through the mesh and tape. This will facilitate removal of staples when replacing the screen.

There is another manual hand fabric stretcher (Frame Fast) which I use all the time. This hand stretcher has rolls of needles that receive the fabric that is tapped on the needles with a brush. (The brush looks like a steel brush only the bristles are made of plastic instead of steel wire.) The fabric is attached to the needles and the handle is pushed down (like the stretcher shown) against the frame to pull and tension the screen. You may use either the stretch cord or staples to tension the screen.

PUT THE SCREEN ON YOUR FRAME

To make sure we are on the same page and understand how we put the screen on the frame, let us go through the steps:

Lay your frame on a flat, sturdy table with the side to be stapled facing up.

Place the screen fabric over the frame allowing at least one inch all around the outside the frame. With scissors (or utility knife) cut or rip screen so that it measures one inch overlap on all four sides.

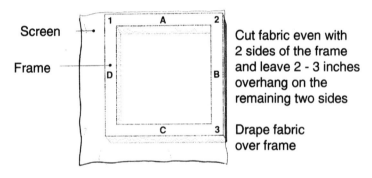

Screen

Frame

Cut fabric even with 2 sides of the frame and leave 2 - 3 inches overhang on the remaining two sides

Drape fabric over frame

Next position screen so that upper left–hand corner of the screen lies on the upper left–hand corner of the frame. The top side of the screen should be parallel to the top of your frame (Side A). Left side of screen should be parallel with left side of frame (Side D). This should give about 2–inch overlap of screen on both the right side (Side B) and the bottom side of your frame (Side C).

With your forefinger and thumb of your left hand hold

screen in place and put four staples at the corners (#1) to hold screen in place.

Now move the screen back to the original position in front of you. Your stitched side (Side A) should be at the top. Make sure the screen along the left side is aligned with the left frame side (Side D). Now with your stretching pliers grasp the overlapping screen at the lower left–hand corner of the frame. Before applying any tension, you should attach a C–clamp or place a weight on the frame at the top.

You will be pulling tension across the frame from the top side (Side A) to the bottom side (Side C). Rotate your tension grip, noting not to tear the screen away from the staples across the top of the frame (Side A). Begin stapling (Side C) the screen left and right angling the staples as you go. You will need to regrip the screen as you now turn the frame so the right side (Side B) is just over the edge of the table. Then grip your overlapped screen with your stretcher pliers and stretch the screen by rotating the head of the pliers against the frame side using a slow downward motion of the handles of your pliers. You may have to use a weight or a large C–clamp to hold the frame in place during the rotating session. Keep an eye on the stapled area (#1) and if the mesh starts to tear, relax the pressure slightly and hold. Check to see that the screen still lies parallel to the frame side (Side A). With alignment checked and tension pressure steady, you are ready to start stapling.

Staple screen to frame at a 30 to 45 degree angle a half–inch apart (for 110 screen). Angling staples this way will permit them to overlap each other and bridge across several mesh threads at a time. (You may need to place staples closer for finer screens.) After a little practice you will see that you can neat "stitch" the screen to the wood frames.

Proceed across the bottom section of your frame. The jaws on your pliers are only 10-inches wide (Your Frame Fast hand stretcher is wider.) so you will need to regrip as the width of the frame dictates.

After you finish stapling the bottom side (Side C) you will move to your left side (Side D). The screen should be lying tight and flat against the frame with the edge of the screen parallel to the frame and no margin outside the frame. At this juncture, you should not need your stretching pliers. Just staple left to right, angling the staples as you go.

Next move to your right side (Side B). Your screen is stretched provided you used steady pressure and moved carefully. The screen should be taut. If the mesh tore or separated at the corners, then you overstretched. (You will have better luck the next time.)

Your screen is now ready for the next step.

The Frame Fast hand fabric stretcher uses an adhesive and activator as its system of bonding screen to the frame. But the stretcher may also be used (as above) with staples or stretch cord.

MESH TENSION

Tight screens print better. That is a fact. Mesh tension provides resistance for the squeegee as it forces the ink onto the substrata (garment) being printed. Whenever the screen is under-stretched, the mesh may move which can smear or blur your image. Under-stretched screen can also lead to picking up ink on the bottom of the screen as it rests on the garment being printed. Even the registration is affected as the mesh rolls under squeegee pressure.

A low-tension screen does not provide any resistance to the squeegee. To compensate, one usually applies more pressure to the squeegee. Too much pressure will shove the ink right on through the garment and onto the platen. And then, the screen must be able to pull back out of the ink. All you really need, if done properly, is to permit enough squeegee pressure to cause the screen to 'kiss, the garment with the ink.

Tension of about 20 Newtons is an average minimum for mesh tension. If you do not have atension meter, you will learn the approximate tension by feel (by trial and error.) A tension meter's main purpose is to help you control the tension of your screen as the screen is being stretched. Not all small shops have one but usually rely on their finger touch and work experience. The fact that they cost between $300 and $400 may also be a factor.

When a screen is over-stretched, it will not return to the neutral position. This further affects the registration for future retentional use of this screen. They also become deformed and will tend to lose tension faster than normal.

In 1996 a national publication estimated that some 70% of all textile print jobs were still being printed with wood frames. So do not become alarmed when you read your next publication that you are crazy for even thinking wood frames.

METAL FRAMES

Now we come to metal frames which are usually square or rectangular aluminum tubing instead of wood. Steel is not used because it would soon rust after so much water exposure during the reclaiming screen process. Aluminum frames usually cost from two to four times as much as wood. frames.

Metal frames usually means that as you stretch the screens,

you will have to use an instant frame adhesive (similar to superglue). You might consider metal frames if you would be printing designs on a thousand shirts. Work that would require forms which must resist moisture and warping.

If you consider investing in metal frames, you may also wish to check into stretching equipment as well. Your supplier dealer can assist you for more information. Keep in mind that metal screens that are constantly reclaimed and used again must also be re-tensioned.

SCREEN STRETCHERS

There are a number of screen stretchers that make it easier to stretch the screen to the right tension on metal frames.

They will each include somewhat the following steps:
1. Place frame inside the stretcher so that frame lines up with the sides of the stretcher.
2. Stretch the screen over the stretcher and lock it in (above the frame).
3. Add a little tension to prevent the fabric from moving.
4. Soften the corners so that it will put tension where the stencil image will be placed on the screen. This will keep the tension in the center of the screen instead of the corners.
5. Stretch all sides a little at a time. Make sure tension is equal in both directions.

6. Once proper tension has been achieved (tension meter or by feel), apply the adhesive to the entire perimeter of the screen sides. (Apply according to manufacturer's instructions.) Some adhesives are supplied with an activator to speed up the drying process. Others simply require that you wait until the adhesive hardens.

7. Once hardened, remove the screen from the stretcher.

8. Trim off the excessive fabric and you are ready for the next step.

Many of the stretchers do not rule out using wood frames or using staples instead of adhesives on wood frames.

There is an adjustable fabric stretcher that is made up of four identical frame sections. Your only tool is a hex wrench which is used to tension the fabric by rotating a roller bar in each of the four frame sections. These frame sections are designed to rest together in a way that they may slide back and forth by using hex wrench. They can adjust to any frame size and require no other tools or bolts. When the right ten sion is achieved, you will be able to use staples or whatever adhesive system you are accustomed to use. The roller diametion size may be 1 1/2" to 2" for general printing including T–shirts.

Rigid wood frames do cost less up front. However, they may need new screen mesh to be attached whenever the tension of the screen drops and begins to affect the quality of your work. Retensionable frames cost more to purchase, but being able to be retensioned a number of times, your screens will last a lot longer. Your potential savings in screen fabric costs as well as savings in production time may make the metal retensionable frames quickly pay for themselves.

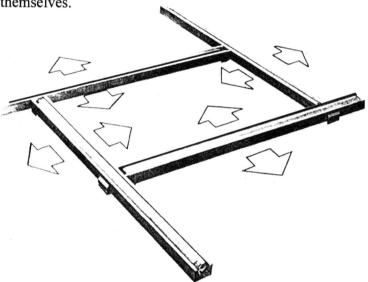

Irish Graphic Products International provides a wealth of information that can be helpful toward making the proper decisions for frames. They may be wood, aluminum, retensionable, prestretched, or custom-made. They offer an entire menu to choose from. They also have supplies that include everything from screen fabric to the complete adhesive system that will make the screen adhere to the frame. I have found them to be friendly and helpful to work with. Their phone number is listed in the appendix. Give them a call.

There are any number of worthwhile makes of retensionable metal frames. It is suggested that you secure literature and additional information from either your supply dealer or the manufacturer. Trade shows provide first-hand look at what is new in the marketplace. These shows also give you the advantage of being able to make first-hand comparisons of the various types of frames. It is not always possible to comparison shop so do the next best thing and have the literature mailed to you.

FOR THE LITTLE GUY

And now for you, the Little Guy, there is an easy to use, retensionable/self-tensioning frame that was introduced just a few years ago. It was called 'THE FRAME., It allows even the most novice of printers to take full advantage of high screen tension without a great deal of practice. I have two of these special frames and am about to invest in an oversized frame to handle the larger magnetic signs I work with.

THE FRAME

Only allen wrench required
Aluminum / Self-Tensioning

They will dry quickly after reclaiming because the open bars allow the water and reclaiming chemicals to escape fast and easily. It features square tube construction and fit easily into any clamping screen printing system. This includes your self-made printer. A quarter-inch allen stretchers, no cords to groove, no staples or liquid adhesives. Easy to stretch or to retension or take down for reclaiming or re-use.

Check out the easy steps that follow.

First lay THE FRAME flat on the table with the fabric side facing up. Take a piece of screen that is 3" to 4" greater than the size of the frame. You lay the screen over the frame so that about 2" hang over each of the four sides.

There will be two clips and four stays furnished with your FRAME. You will need to match the length of each stay with the bar you are working with.

Place the clips into the slot of side #1 about an inch from each end. Begin sliding the stay into the slot, a little at a time, while pulling screen in the opposite direction you are sliding the stay. You will remove each clip as you come to each one. Each stay should extend slightly past the bar you are working on.

Next, you turn the frame around as you prepare to work on the opposite side. Pull the screen tight toward you and insert the two clips as you did above and repeat the process of inserting the clips and stay.

of inserting the clips and stay.

You will proceed and follow the above steps with each of sides #3 and #4.

The next step is to take the quarter-inch allen wrench (furnished) and begin with side #1 and rotate the wrench two notches. Do this all around each corner until the entire frame is wider in both directions. Then let THE FRAME set for 15 minutes to let your work 'harden.,

After 15 minutes, repeat the entire process (again two notches all way around) and wait for another 15 minutes. Each two notches tighten the screen approximately 1/4" each direction. Three times around and the screen should achieve the desired tension. You will need to work out the perfect feel. It will come quickly after your first few tries.

A rough sketch follows to help make it easier to understand.

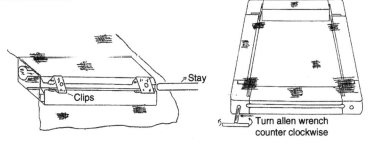

Stay

Clips

Turn allen wrench counter clockwise

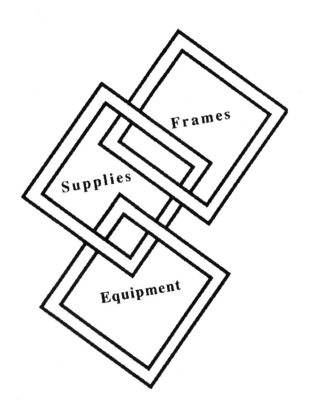

Frames

Supplies

Equipment

CHAPTER 3

EMULSION

The choices for making the screen stencils have been limited primarily to:

1. A two-part liquid direct emulsion (Diazo) and
2. Capillary film (to be taken up separately)

Most printers to-date have usually stuck with the system they learned during their introductory screen printing experience. They are reluctant to change. For most small print shops, that means the diazo process.

In a recent survey by a national printwear magazine, a majority chose the diazo. The deciding issues included relative costs, speed of operation, consistency, durability and flexibility. All considered, the two-part diazo system is destined to continue with printwear operations for sometime to come.

DIRECT EMULSION

Dirasol 914 is a diazo-photopolymer direct emulsion product that I have used for ten years. It has good resolution and excellent definition. It has worked well for me. It combines the best of diazo and photopolymer chemistry. It has excellent resistance to solvents (inks, cleaners, etc.). Dirasol is fast-drying, non-polluting and is biodegradable.

At this point, bear in mind that we want to achieve three things with the screen:

1. First we need an emulsion or film to adhere to the screen.

2. Then, we need to be able to reproduce a printable image onto the screen.

3. And finally, the screen needs to provide a flat surface to hold the ink for printing on the garment.

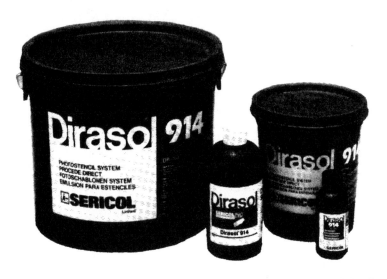

The Diazo has to be mixed with a sensitizer (furnished). Once mixed, it has a pot-life of about six months when refrigerated. At room temperature the pot-life is cut in two, only about three months.

This emulsion is available in either clear or blue. Clear makes it easier to register screens when on the press. Blue emulsion turns to green color once it is fully mixed with the sensitizer. Colored emulsion is easier to spot pin holes and other imperfections in the screen when the screen is checked out against a bright light.

Mixing the emulsion with the sensitizer is a comparatively easy task, especially when attaching a paint mixing blade on your hand drill. You can complete the mixing operation in five minutes or so in this manner.

Screens coated with emulsion can be stored in a cool, dry and safe (light-free) environment for up to two months.

Once the emulsion has been sensitized, it should be allowed to stand for 45 minutes to an hour before use. This is to allow any air bubbles introduced during the mixing operation to come to the top and escape.

An added note – once the emulsion is sensitized, it should be mixed before each use to ensure that the sensitizer is evenly distributed in the emulsion. Then allow another fifteen minutes to elapse to get rid of any additional air bubbles. A wood paint paddle or plastic spatula can do the job during subsequent mixing.

The screen must be absolutely dry before coating with the

liquid emulsion.

COATING APPLICATION

There are several ways to apply emulsion to a screen. A coating trough, more often called a scoop coater, is easy to handle and lightweight. It has a smooth rounded edge to allow sufficient emulsion to be deposited onto the screen. It has been designed to produce an even-coated screen. It can stand upright between coats. Most will hold enough emulsion to handle several screens without refilling. The coater has tight fitting plastic end caps that serve as guides to keep the correct angle during coating.

You can also use a flat plastic spreader. Even a piece of stiff cardboard could work in an emergency. As long as the emulsion is spread evenly over the screen, there is no problem how it is coated onto the screen.

HOW TO COAT A SCREEN

1. Degrease the screen, rinse, and let dry in an enclosed place free from dust and any airborne particles discussed earlier.
2. Prepare the liquid emulsion according to the manufacturers instructions.
3. Coat under safelight (yellow light) – avoid fluorescent lights, mercury vapor bulbs, and natural daylight. These

light sources will expose your emulsion.

4. Make sure your coating equipment is clean – your scoop coater, squeegee, or spreader blade.

5. Make sure the emulsion is blended evenly and allowed to stand 15 minutes before filling your scoop coater.

6. With one hand, tilt the screen and with the scoop coater in other hand begin casting back side of screen (side of screen that will be in contact with garment).

7. As the coater reaches near the top of the screen, tip the screen forward and complete the coating stroke. This will keep the emulsion from dripping as you remove the scoop coater. If you are using scraper blade, you will be making several passes using the blade as your scooper. Make sure it is done evenly and completely.

8. Turn the screen around and repeat the above procedure on the inside of the screen (Squeegee side). If it appears that your strokes (either scoop or blade) were not smooth, apply a second coat.With a little practice, either procedure will become easy to do.

9. After the screen has been coated on both sides, place the screen in a drying position. If you plan having a drying cabinet, place in the cabinet with garment-side down. Or you can build a cabinet with racks to hold screens horizontal. I have added a regular fan to hasten drying time. Remember – KEEP DUST FREE!

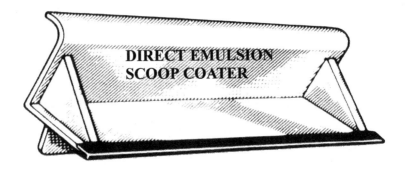

CAPILLARY FILM

Capillary films are pre-sensitized emulsion films applied to a wet screen before exposure. The capillary properties cause the film to thoroughly adhere to any fabric (including metal).

For preparing capillary film, you must first begin with a clean, tensioned, degreased screen.

Next, cut the film to the correct screen size. Film may be ordered by rolls or in sheets. Precut sheets are much easier to work with and probably will have less waste during the preparation process.

Thoroughly wet the screen with a wetting agent (water). Allow the screen to stand in a vertical position while you roll the film onto the screen. With the emulsion side out, touch the film's edge at the top of the screen and roll down evenly.

34

When the water dries, the polyester backing is peeled away and the screen is ready for print. If the backing does not immediately peel away, the screen may not be totally dry.

Unexposed stencils can be stored for weeks under proper conditions.

Capillary films have a toughness and durability similar to direct emulsions. Once they are properly adhered to the screen and dried, the clear plastic removed, the screens are processed just like direct emulsion. Both produce high quality stencils. Both are light sensitive emulsions. They are exposed to ultraviolet light for a specified period of time and then developed when washed out with water.

Safelight illumination is recommended while working with either method. This usually means yellow light conditions (even a yellow bug light will work).

PROCESS CAPILLARY FILM

Begin by taping the film positive (art transparency) to the emulsion side of the film (print side). You should already have removed the clear backing when the screen is dry.

Center the screen on the glass exposure unit. (See next chapter.) Cover the screen (black cloth) and set the timer for the correct exposure. (It is a good idea to get a kitchen timer at department or hardware store.)

Once the timer alerts you that the exposure is complete, turn off the equipment. Take exposed screen out, peel away the transparency, and then do the washout. Wet both sides of the screen with water spray. Garden hose, bathtub, or sink O.K. With capillary stencil you will do most of the washout on the print side (garment side). As with direct emulsion screens, you can hold the screen up to the light and inspect your work after each washout. Dry the screen in a dust-free cabinet. Then the screens can be hardened by exposing them to sunlight or high-powered UV light or simply stored in a dry, dust-free cabinet.

Most all printwear suppliers will have both capillary film and direct emulsions as they represent different manufacturing companies. Most have technicians readily available who can supply answers to problems as they pertain to their products. Each will furnish regular literature that pertains to preparation, shelf life, and usage.

ROLL DOWN METHOD:

Throughly wet the screen in vertical position. Roll the film sheet emulsion side out, around the plastic tube provided. Touch the film edge to the top of the screen and roll down evenly, Wipe off excess water around film and frame. If air bubbles are present, spray, then squeegee mesh.

Both types of emulsions strive to provide the best possible results in the preparation of direct photostencils used in screen printing. You have a right to be seeking a fast-exposing, solvent and humidity resistant direct emulsion. And, of course, you need reclaimability of the screens. Added note: You need to blockout open area in fabric between frame and stencil. Paper tape is best for use with all types of ink except water based, for "ink proofing" the frame. If taped properly, ink will not leak from frame.

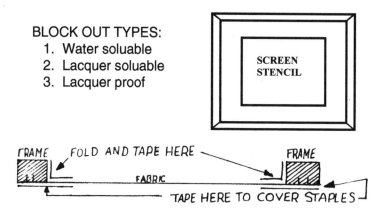

BLOCK OUT TYPES:
1. Water soluable
2. Lacquer soluable
3. Lacquer proof

SCREEN STENCIL

FRAME   FOLD AND TAPE HERE   FRAME
FABRIC
TAPE HERE TO COVER STAPLES

EXPOSURE BOX

You can purchase your exposure equipment directly from the manufacturer or from most any of your regular silk screen suppliers. Many screen print suppliers may represent one or more manufacturers of printing equipment. The exposure unit is expensive. However, if you are in a hurry to get started and can stand the cost, it is convenient way to hasten your shop into production.

Or you can make your own exposure box. I did and still use it. Here below are the plans you can use to build your own. Your cost should be $100 or so.

Your box will be 24"x30"x9" deep with a plate glass cover. Your material list includes:

Floor of box – 1/2" or 3/4" plywood – size 24"x30" (Particle board will be fine.)

Walls of box – (2 pcs.) 9"x22 1/2"x 3/4" thick pine shelving (for two end pieces)

(2 pcs.) 9"x30"x 3/4" thick pine shelving (for 2 sides)

Lighting – Need (2) 24" double fixture unfiltered blacklight fluorescent tubes

Assemble the sides and ends to the floor (plywood or particle board). Simply screw or nail the parts together.

Lay out the double fixture fluorescent lights. Complete the wiring after you center the fixtures and screw into place. You will need an electrical cord to extend from the exposure box to the wall outlet. You probably should add an 'on-and-off, switch for convenience.

Your local electrical supply house can secure your unfiltered fluorescent lights. Make sure that your electrical supplier understands the type of fluorescent system you need. They are similar to the "grow lights", your mother uses for her house plants. These lights may look like the regular fluorescent lights but they produce an ultraviolet light that your exposure box requires for converting your artwork transparencies into screen copy. This is essential.

A discount lumber yard can supply your framing needs plus the nails/screws you require. You may find a piece of plate glass (24 1/2"x30 1/2") from a glass company or maybe a salvage dealer. Tape the edges of the glass with duck tape to prevent cuts while handling the glass. This tape will also add a little extra security when cleaning or when removing the glass for servicing the lights.

Keep the glass clean and clear to prevent any pin holes from developing by dust particles.

EXPOSURE BOX

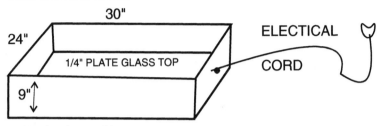

Build simple wood box.

ADD 24"
DOUBLE FIXTURE
UNFILTERED BLACKLIGHT
FLUORESCENT

FROM THE TOP IT
LOOKS LIKE THIS

Place exposure box on table convenient to get to but out of the way of normal screen printing production.

CHAPTER 4
ARTWORK

Most all silk screening begins with artwork. You see something in the newspaper or magazine and immediately imagine the subject matter being transferred to a T–shirt. It may become a fad if it has something that will remain public for a time. Or it may be something worth making a statement about. By putting it on a T–shirt and being seen by others, a statement is being made, like a billboard for all to notice.

Marathons, athletic activities, rock concerts are popular events that are naturally attractive for T–shirts and caps. They all begin with the message or artwork. Everyone has seen them at one time or other. Picture a runner with the name of the 5K or 10K run. Find the sponsor and try to secure the account. Every school and little league team shows team spirit by sporting the name across the front or back of a T–shirt, sweatshirt, or jacket.

Today the PC (personal computer) has become the fastest and easiest way to prepare one's artwork. If you do not own or know how to operate a personal computer, get acquainted with someone who does. Tell him or her what you have in mind. If you are dealing with someone in business, he will have a business card, stationary, brochure, etc. and most likely some idea what is needed on his garment. He wants to advertise his firm or business. Schools or sporting events also have ideas of what they would like to imprint. You can take these ideas to your computer printer (or future associate) and sketch an outline of the print art, logo, or related subject layout.

Computer graphics can become the screen printer's miracle worker. With the proper software, the computer can combine the skills of an artist with the fonts and lettering of a printer and sketch the layout to make your T–shirt or cap stand out. As a screen printer you are now a specialist. With the computer (again with proper software) you have numberless types of lettering available. If you are using someone to do your computer work, you will need to help train him/her to make the computer jump through the routines that will enhance your artwork. To make letters stand out you can make one large letter overshadow a small word . ARKLA Or maybe a vertical layout $\begin{smallmatrix}A\\S\\U\end{smallmatrix}$ or arc large letters like . ASU Start practicing on scratch pads the different ways you can layout letters.

Begin analyzing the T–shirts and caps you see people wearing. Look at the ads that appear in the newspapers and magazines. Try to see how a business could use your services by placing a logo on a T–shirt or the store's aprons, even something as simple as just their name across a cap.

There are clip art booklets that are available for reproducing artwork at no cost other than the price of the booklet. These are most often ad slicks that are readily reproduced with part of your complete artwork. They are available in many categories such as sporting figures, mascots, logos, and much, much, more. (See appendix.)

In recent years there have been an increasing number of computer operators going into their own business of desktop publishing. With more and better sophisticated software programs for graphic designs, screenprinters have less to fear in the transition from traditional hand-created artwork to that of computer-generated art. Talk to those who work with computers. They can help you better understand how a computer can help you become more productive and efficient. Trade magazines also help you keep abreast of how computers are being used in other printwear shops.

I began laying out the artwork I needed for T–shirts, caps, and jackets by using glue sticks and paper cutouts of clip art. I would sketch the lettering around the rest of artwork using a black marking pen. This became the rough draft given to the instant print shop. The operator would scan in the logo art and then computer type the rest. In a short time we both learned about each other and a better understanding how the computer could provide what we needed.

It became sort of 1, 2, 3-approach to designing either a cap or T–shirt layout.

First visualize an arc over the logo. The balance of the copy area is spread out under the logo area.

Second, add the logo (picture, mascot, etc.).

Finally, complete the advertising, address, phone number copy.

There follows a series of actual art layouts for T–shirts.
Think how they could have been designed differently.

HERE IS YOUR PROCEDURE FOR YOUR FIRST T–SHIRT:

1. Layout a rough sketch of what is to be printed (e.g., ABC Company).

2. Have print shop print out your artwork for approval. After approval is given, have your printer prepare a positive transparency.

   > Note: Positive, as opposed to negative, will imprint black dye on clear sheet of plastic. Transparencies are available from local business office supply store.

3. Size of transparency is for T–shirt so it will be 8 1/2"x11" size. This will be used to make screen on exposure box. Make screen –Select 110 mesh.

   > Select frame for T–shirt screen.
   > Cut mesh to size – allow 2" all around.
   > Tension screen to frame – Staple, rope, or adhesive.
   > Apply Diazo direct emulsion to screen.
   > Allow screen to dry and store until ready to make screen image.

5. Center transparency on the glass top of exposure box and align screen frame properly on transparency. Set clock timer for proper exposure.

   Note: You will need to experiment with the time requirement. My timing has been 8 1/2 minutes with the

exposure lamps being 8 inches below my artwork
(transparency). Use safelight conditions while handling
screen.

6. After timer signals, wash exposed screen with water
spray from your sink (or tub) or even outside faucet.
Keep lights to a minimum if use outside faucet. (Best to
do after sunset to minimize sunlight. Cloudy days work
well for me.)

7. Dry the screen.

8. Block out all pin holes, fish eyes or exposed emulsion
mistakes.

9. Tape both sides of screen to prevent any possible ink
leakage onto your garment.

10. Select your plastisol ink for the job. Use a clean
squeegee. Test your first impression on old newspaper.
Evaluate your work before placing your T–shirt on the
press.

CHAPTER 5

PLASTISOL INK

Most articles about plastisol inks begin with a statement that plastisol inks are the most widely used inks in the textile industry. They are the most popular because they are easy to work with, do not dry up on the screen, can become very opaque on dark garments and generally will work well on practically any garment material you plan to print on. All ink companies make an all-purpose plastisol ink.

Technically, plastisols are made of plasticizers and polyvinyl chloride resins (PVC).

Plastisols can be used virtually on any substrate since the substrate can withstand the curing temperature (320°F) and the surface of the substrate is porous enough to allow the ink to penetrate. Since it has no real adhesive power, plastisol inks cannot work on plastic, metal or glass. They will not work on waterproofed nylon without a special bonding (catalyst) agent.

Plastisol inks will not air-dry like most inks do. You may leave them uncapped in the can or left on the screen for days (even months) and still they will not dry up or clog your screen.

Plastisol ink will only cure when heat is applied. Plastisol will become soft to the touch (also called gelled or semi-cured) between 180°F and 250°F. It becomes fully cured between 280°F and 320°F. It is practically impossible to overcure plastisol since curing temperature is already beyond the scorching point of the garment.

Most believe that plastisol must be brought to the full cure temperature and held there for two or three minutes to attain a full cure. However, in commercial use, plastisol is generally cured in an infrared curing oven that operates at a much higher temperature. Once the ink reaches the proper cure temperature it becomes a continuous film and is fully cured. That means it can be cured within a few seconds if the ink is not too thick and the temperature is high enough. If the plastisol does not reach the right curing temperature, it will be undercured and the ink will crack and flake off the garment. An actual wash is the best test (not always available or feasible). There is another, more practical way to detect a possible undercure. Simply stretch the print and if it cracks badly and does not retract, it is probably undercured. Most likely there is a need to increase the temperature by increasing the time under the heating element.

DRYING METHODS

The hobbyist may use simple methods to dry the printed

work. I have used a shirt heat press (described in more detail under equipment), a small home oven, hair dryer, and heat lamps. Also a flash curing unit can be helpful, especially when printing wet on wet designs on T–shirts or other garments. The flash curing unit is also helpful on drying nylon jackets.

Small commercial dryers are becoming less costly and available for small shops. Be aware that temperatures must reach 300°F to 320°F for most multi-purpose plastisol imprints.

My shirt heat press has a thermometer that I set at 375°F, then pull the press down within 2-3" of the garment for 20-25 seconds. A sheet of teflon and a sheet of transfer paper are set on top of the garment. Then I set the press down on top of this teflon under pressure for 4-5 seconds. This not only irons the garment and smooths the wrinkles, but also ensures total cure. This process has worked well for me over the years. I still see some of my T–shirts being worn after eight or nine years. This attests to the fact that the print is washable and that it was totally cured as well.

With plastisol inks you can print direct from the can. You would like it thick and heavy for work on dark garments and creamy and smooth for light garments. You can use a viscosity reducer if it is too heavy. Paint thinner can be used to thin but keep in mind that it may also affect the washabil ity of the printed area. So be careful with the paint thinners.

Most any screen mesh can be used with plastisol inks. Depending on what is being printed, the mesh range will be between 85 and 160. Refer to screen mesh chapter.

Each supply dealer will have several catalog pages devoted specifically to plastisol inks. First they tell you what it is and how easy it is to work with. Then they may take up ten or more pages telling you all about inks that they have designed for specialized printing work.

For most printing jobs an all-purpose plastisol should work well. I started with quarts of red, white, royal, black and a quart of white nylon (with catalyst). That worked well until I was given a special 4–color T–shirt job. It required three additional colors . . . fluorescent pink, yellow, and pink. I thought I needed the job to break in my 4–color printer! I was introduced quickly to the problems of printing wet on wet, imprinting on dark garments, and perfect registration of colors. I would have been better off without the work but it turned into a learning experience. Some of the fluorescent ink is still around and usable.

I also picked up an old Toastmaster broiler oven. I removed the oven door. With the temperature set at 375°F or so, I have used the oven for drying caps, mousepads, posters, transfers, decals, and can coolers. A flash curing unit has been used to semi-cure nylon jackets for easier handling off the press. Also I use the flash curing unit whenever multicolor printing requires wet on wet process.

PUFF INK

Puff ink is a plastisol ink and is fairly easy to work with. Puff ink expands when heated during the drying process. I have had good results with 110 mesh even though puff ink is thicker than regular plastisol inks. Keep in mind that the expansion of puff ink will have an effect on your art work. Fine lines and lettering will close when drying. Heavy black lettering will thicken so should be reduced with puff ink.

NYLON INK

The manufacturers make a special nylon ink that is somewhat thicker than the regular plastisol ink and is used for printing on nylon jackets. To become effective you will need to add a catalyst (bonding agent) to the nylon ink. The liquid catalyst may be ordered separately but is included when specifically ordering nylon ink. I have used regular plastisol ink and always added a little additional catalyst to the ink when I do. The manufacturer will instruct properly mixing of the two.

If I have a half-dozen nylon jackets to print, I usually take a small putty knife (tablespoon amount) and count out seven globs of ink into a clean cup. This is for six jackets plus one for the screen. My ratio of catalyst is 10 to 1. So I add one tablespoon of catalyst, mix, and stir. As you stir, you will note the mixture begins to thin somewhat. If you have added too much of the bonding agent and made the mix too thin, set it aside for an hour or so and it will thicken up. If I use regular plastisol, I normally will add a little additional catalyst to be doubly sure the ink will adhere to the jacket.

The reason for the catalyst (bonding agent) is that the nylon weave is so tight that the plastisol ink will not adhere and will flake off when dried. The catalyst holds the ink in place and makes it more durable.

Another thing to remember is once the ink and bonding agents are mixed, the pot life of the mixture is reduced to around eight to ten hours. Consequently, you should only mix up what you plan on using. Any left over from the job will harden up and will be tossed away. A putty knife can remove the ink after it has hardened. The cup used for mixing can be cleaned with paint thinner and used again.

I have used 110 to 160 mesh for printing jackets. I use a flash curing portable heating unit to fast cure the jacket before removing from the press. Then it is placed on the shirt heat press. The heating element is drawn down within six to seven inches of the printed jacket. With the tempera ture of 375°F, each jacket is allowed to remain on the shirt press for approximately two minutes. This will cure the plastisol. The bonding agent will continue its hardening process for another day or two.

Before printing a jacket, I normally place a protective sheet of teflon over the jacket and run a heated household iron over the area to be printed. This not only smooths out the jacket, but also makes it easier to print. This is especially true when printing nylon quilted jackets.

Most nylon jackets are waterproofed which can affect any suitable printing. To be on the safe side, you can wipe the printing area with rubbing alcohol. Jacket manufacturers usually inform jacket buyers which of their jackets are waterproofed. So if waterproofed, apply the alcohol.

WASH-UP
Remove all excess ink with help of squeegee and putty knife and put back into the ink container. You can then wash the screen with paint thinner (mineral spirits) and heavy duty paper towels from auto department of your local department or hardware store. You can also use old T–shirt rejects in your wash-up. Old rags from garage sales are also a cheap way to clean screens. Clean your screens

immediately after every job. It makes for easier reclaiming later. It also promotes a clean work area.

Note: Nylon ink mixed with catalyst cannot be saved. Discard.

WATER-BASED INK

Water-based inks have improved dramatically over recent years. They have their place in the printing industry along with the plastisol inks.

Most screenprinters have cut their teeth with plastisol and many are still unwilling to recognize the various advantages of water-based inks. Water-based inks require more stringent controls to achieve maximum production and quality. Plastisol is more forgiving and lets the screen printer get by with many practices that would not be acceptable with water-based inks.

Water-based inks can be printed on many, if not all, of the substrates that will accept plastisol inks. This includes paper, cardboard, vinyls, plastics, cottons, cotton/poly blends, and a variety of other fabrics.

Use of water-based ink requires a different way of thinking as compared to plastisol. Water-based inks tend to evaporate where plastisol does not. For example, there is a need for faster production required for use of water-based ink. This is due to the ink's tendency to dry out when left exposed, whether in the can but especially on the screen. With plastisol, you can leave it on the screen for days (or even months) and come back and start again from where you left off.

With water-based inks, colors that overlap one another will blend into a new color. This is critical when your artwork calls for precise 'butt-registration on the printed garment. You may be achieving a color not intended with your artwork.

Proper preparation of screens is the same for water-based inks and plastisols. That simply pertains to de-hazing, degreasing, retensioning screens, and keeping them dust-free.

Make certain that you use an emulsion specified for water-based ink. You could use the same type of emulsion with plastisol ink. But your plastisol type of emulsion will not work with water-based ink. It would break down under the abrasiveness of water.

Water-based inks also require a change to a water-resistant blockout in keeping with the change of emulsion. If tape is used, it must be waterproof tape as well.

For water-based screen mesh selection, use this general rule of thumb:

1. For towels, sleepwear – 110
2. For T–shirts, athletic wear – 160
3. For fine-knit, 100% polyester – 200-220

Some believe that water-based inks offer environmental benefits over plastisol inks. But if you check this out, you may find that the claim is more of a smokescreen for marketing water-based inks than based on facts. But even so, some screen printing shops promote the environmental image because they use water-based inks. Most customers don't know the difference.

CURE FOR WATER-BASED INKS

Most suppliers recommend that water-based inks be dried at 300°F for three minutes to achieve full cure. Many small shops will not have a large dryer designed to cure water-based inks. This may require additional passes through smaller dryer units. It will require some testing to ensure desired results.

Being water-based, the garments may also be air-dried over an extended period of time. You can test for results after 45 minutes to an hour.

Water-based inks have a much shorter shelf-life than do plastisols. A can of water-based ink may last a month if sealed since bacteria grow in water-based substances.

Because of this, most companies are adding an anti-fungus ingredient to promote a longer shelf-life. Plastisol can last for five to six years or more.

Another point to remember, just because it is water-based, you cannot simply pour the waste down the drain. Chemicals in the inks, such as pigments, stabilizers, fungicides, resin, and the like can contaminate the water. You will need to filter out the undesirables and dispose of them through hazardous waste procedures. The same safety precautions should follow wastes resulting from use of plastisols.

WATER-BASED-INK ADVANTAGES/DISADVANTAGES

In summary, here are a few of the advantages and disadvantages of water-based inks.

1. Softhand. The chief reason for water-based ink is the naturally soft dye-like hand (or feel). This is especially felt when feeling the printing on towels, sleepwear and fashion apparel.
2. Dry-cleanability. Once fully dried, most water-based inks are dry-cleanable. Plastisols are soluble in chlorinated solvents used in dry cleaning and so cannot tolerate dry cleaning.
3. Ironability. Water-based inks are tolerant of heat and can be ironed. Again, this makes them especially suitable for fashion apparel. Plastisol inks will melt and

smear when exposed to sufficient heat. If there is a need to iron out wrinkles on plastisol, turn garment inside out and iron with teflon sheet.

4. Penetration. Water-based inks are ideal for printing on materials that require penetration into the substrate such as terry cloth towels. On the other hand, plastisol will tend to lie on the surface of the towels.

5. Drying. Plastisols require only heat to become wash-fast. Water-based ink systems require a process that must remove all of the solvent (that is water). They may feel dry but usually require actual wash test on products to be sure all moisture has been removed.

6. Screen Clogging. Unlike plastisols, water-based inks clog up as they dry in the screen. You will need to water spray and continuous action to keep the screen printable.

7. Opacity. One of the downfalls of water-based inks is their lack of opacity. They may be brilliant on white and pastel garments but are least effective on dark. T–shirts and other garments.

8. Odor. Water-based ink system has a post-processing odor that results when the chemical reaction to heat produces sulfur dioxide. This rotten egg smell will be irritating unless the print shop is well ventilated.

Water-based ink systems have been designed to fit almost any printer's need. However, plastisols are more forgiving in this use and especially for the beginner. Most printers who have used water-based ink report that they are no more difficult to work with than plastisols. The manufacturers are working to overcome the initial disadvantages of water-based ink, namely the drying and clogging on the screens. They are beginning to offer ready-to-use inks that do not require additives. Both systems will provide plenty of work for the serious-minded screen printer of the future. The dealer or distributor representatives will be glad to supply additional information for those who seek it.

COLOR WHEEL

While on the subject of ink, here is a note about colors of ink. There will be times when a client will want a specific color of ink to be printed on his cap or garment. A quart of plastisol ink will cost between $20 and $25 (including shipping and handling). Look over the colors of ink on hand and if you have a color wheel, you might consider mixing two or more inks to come up with the desired color. You can alert your customer that it might cost additionally to order the special ink color wanted. That would be the best procedure to follow. If not, consider mixing inks and add a cover charge.

Color wheels may be purchased from most any art supply store or check it out with your supply dealer.

Red, yellow, and blue are primary colors. Secondary colors are the mixture of two primary colors. For example, when you add red to yellow you get orange. Or when adding yellow to blue, you get green.

Then you can get an intermediate color when mixing a primary color with a secondary color. For example, mix blue with green to get teal.

You can play with the color wheel for more color combinations. As you experiment with mixtures be sure to record how each color has been achieved.

You can begin with a formula of four tablespoons of base mixed with 1/16 teaspoon of color.

CHAPTER 6

ADHESIVES

TYPES OF ADHESIVES

There are three types of adhesives that will be taken up separately:

1. There is a powdered transfer adhesive that comes in a shaker can. This will be used for making transfers for caps, sweaters or other hard to transfer material.

2. There is a table adhesive for textiles that comes in an aerosol spray can. This can be used on the platen to hold garments from moving while being printed. It can also be used on glass, paper and other surfaces for temporary bonds. It can hold transfer paper while being printed.

3. And there are adhesives for attaching the screen mesh to the frame.

   These adhesives will be taken up in reverse order.

FRAME ADHESIVE

The screen frame must be clean and free of all dirt, grease or any other contaminates that may interfere with a good adhering of the mesh to the frame. Wooden frames should be sanded and be free of old paint and the like. Metal frames need to be clean so that no foreign agents will interfere with the adhesive. Since the adhesive will stick to the first thing it contacts, it is very important that the screen be tightly attached to the frame as well.

With the screen tensioned tightly over the frame, check to be sure that the screen has intimate contact everywhere over the frame. Now you can apply a bead of adhesive all around the frame. Then with a small applicator or squeegee, spread the adhesive the width of the frame. After initial spread, apply additional adhesive to any missed or weak spots.

First make sure the frame is clean. Then apply an unbroken line of adhesive along the frame.

You should get between 60 70 frame feet per ounce of adhesive

Spread adhesive with applicator. Some frame materials, like new wood tend to soak up adhesive the first time you apply it.

Press lightly with fingertips on center of screen to pull fabric tight against frame.

Spray frame evenly with Activator from a distance of 8-12". Adhesive will turn dull when cured. spray lightly. Too much Activator will boil adhesive and weaken the bond. Activator will not clog screen.

Next, spray the activator lightly onto the adhesive. Remember that there will be no bond without the activator. Cure time will be rapid, in approximately three to ten seconds, depending on the thickness of the adhesive plus the temperature of the frame. Take care not to spray too much activator as it will weaken the bond.

There is a safety solvent designed to dissolve any cured adhesive from one's fingers, hands, or work area, should any accidental bonding take place. There is a cured adhesive remover that comes in larger containers.

To remove the fabric from the frame when ready, simply lift one corner and begin to pull it back from the frame. Once done, your frame is ready for reuse.

Like all chemicals, read and follow the instructions supplied by the manufacturer.

If you plan to use staples or rope to tension your screen, of course, you would have no need for this adhesive.
Refer to section on adhesives in frame section.

SPRAY TABLE ADHESIVE
There is a table adhesive for textiles. It comes in an aerosol spray can. It is sprayed onto the platen on the press to hold T–shirts and other garments in place while printing.

It may be used on glass, paper, and other surfaces for temporary or permanent bonds. It is also used to hold transfer paper in place while printing transfers. Spray lightly so as to not get too much of adhesive on back of each transfer.

TRANSFER ADHESIVE

This is a heat activated powder applied to the wet printed transfer. It is used to increase the plastisol's transferability to caps and other hard to transfer material. It comes in a one-pound shaker can. Larger refills are also available.

Shake a small amount of the powder into a pile on a sheet of paper. Old folded newspaper works well. Hold edge of newspaper in one hand, direct the transfer in under the powder. Be sure to cover the entire printed area. Then shake off excess powder. Be sure to keep the powder on the newspaper. No messes, please.

These transfers are now ready to be partially cured for five or six seconds under oven heat. If sticky to touch, add another second or two. They can now be stacked or ready for use to be transferred to a cap, garment or be shipped or stored.

Transfers can be stored indefinitely. Keep away from heat.

Perhaps one of the easiest ways to get into silk screening is to learn how to apply transfers to caps and T–shirts. There are a number of transfer companies who will sell with no minimum and in small quantities. The major problem is to know what will sell and of course how many? Your only equipment to start this way would be a cap heat press and a T–shirt heat press.

Or you can go another step, make your own screen press and prepare your own transfers.

Transfers present a way to be prepared for taking care of a large number attending an event but can minimize any risk and inventory by just preprinting a few in advance. Having the transfers available, you can print at the location and not lose any large number of sales. However, if you preprinted a great number of shirts or caps and the event was canceled, you could be stuck with large inventory of unwanted shirts and caps. It becomes even greater should a date be preprinted and the tournament becomes postponed due to inclement weather.

SOME ADVANTAGES

•With transfers, there is no need to decide in advance what shirt colors or sizes to stock.

•Low overhead. Your only investment would be the number of transfers, some T–shirts and a transfer press. •Small risk. Should rain cancel an event or the design is rejected, the investment would be minimal when compared to having preprinted the total anticipated inventory of shirts.

Here is an idea you can run with. Take a generic fishing stock transfer and customize it with a name added to the shirt. Now take a dozen or so of these shirts to a local tackle shop to retail. Or some other stock item retailing to tourist trade, add a name and sell just a few at a time. You can do this when you only have to purchase a few at a time. Or buy a few more and set up for more than one client. When you add a name to customize a stock design, you can multiply potential clients.

For making my own transfers, I have used regular plastisol ink with 110 screen mesh. If I were to consider contract printing for others, I would recommend a vinyl-type transfer ink and go with 86 screen mesh.

There is a heat tape that I use to hold the transfer in place when placed on the cap heat press.

There are two basic types of transfer:
1. A hot split transfer is usually applied at 375° to 400°F for eight to twelve seconds with firm pressure and then peeled off (hot) immediately. Try to remove the transfer paper off the garment in one smooth continuous motion after releasing pressure of the heat press. The ink will split leaving the transferred image on the garment and a noticeable ink film on the transfer paper. That is how it got its

name "Hot Split." These are the most popular transfers used for T–shirts.

2. A cold peel transfer is applied with somewhat cooler temperature for a longer time — at 350°F for 10 to 15 seconds with firm pressure. The transfer is allowed to cool while rubbing it with a cloth. (Like ironing the transfer with cloth instead of an iron.) After cooling, peel off the transfer paper. All the ink is left on the garment and the transfer paper is clean.

There are literally tons of heat transfers to choose from should you gather catalogs from all suppliers. The biggest problem, of course, is choosing which ones will sell. Once these are applied to a T–shirt, the shirt cannot be used for any other purpose. But there are unlimited marketing possibilities once you begin to understand their best uses and remain within your investment budget. Whatever you do, don't forget to follow the instruction furnished by your manufacturer.

Christmas time is a good time to check out transfers. Most everyone is in the holiday spirit and do not mind showing off their feelings with a T–shirt or sweatshirt. Since you can purchase these transfers in small quantities and can have multiple options to sell over a period of time, this could be a worthwhile endeavor to check out. Remember also, that transfers do not require artwork, no screens to make or reclaim. All you do is supply the shirt and transfer onto the shirt.

Many professional athletic teams license their logos now. Securing transfers is an easy way to secure license to market these special logos as well as an easy way to create and sell your garment. These transfers offer a cost-efficient and quick alternative to T–shirt printing.

Do your homework on any civic, school, or charitable activities in your area. Plan ahead and get a jump ahead on your competition. Contact every transfer manufacturer and get on their mailing list. Thousands of ideas will explode as you look over their catalogs. These are readily available with just a phone call. Don't drop the phone!

MAKE YOUR OWN TRANSFER

Transfer sheets of size 11"x13" cost about 8 cents each. You can make cap transfers for less than a penny each. Or you can make transfers for youth T–shirts for around a nickel. Then an adult size would be less than a dime.

Remember what was said about plastisol inks. These are partial dried at 180° to 250°F for six to seven seconds. Then the full cure takes place on the garment at 280° to 320°F. You may have to experiment with your time but you can start checking out at ten seconds or so.

Many suppliers will send you free samples of their transfers. Test them out on your equipment and on your rags. This is a good way to begin.

Here is a good way to reduce risk and inventory. If your customer wants date and year to show for a tournament, but does not want to get stuck with a lot of dated garments, how about making the transfer (or have them made) and then only make a few at a time. If these average only $1 or $2 apiece, they become a practical and economical choice for those looking for a low capital investment.

Early in my screen printing experience, I attended a Karate tournament. I had about 120 transfers each for two different layouts (120 all total) along with my trusty shirt heat press. It was a bad day but I sold nearly 60 finished T–shirts. The transfers were still good. My partner made a good deal with the promoter after the tournament and the balance of the transfers were sold. Had all been transferred to T–shirts, there could have been a waste. The promoter thought he had a better deal and it was easier to sell. Both parties won.

With quick turnarounds and receiving shipments almost overnight, there is little need to keep a large transfer inventory. Smaller inventories will provide greater financial flexibility and allow you to better control your costs.

Keep your transfer stored at room temperature. Keep them in plastic bags and store with original instructions. It would be best to start organizing these transfers early. Store them by category or by numbers.

Shirt heat press transfer machine
Courtesy National Screen Printing Equip.

You should know what type of garment or product the transfer will be used on. Will it be 100% cotton, T-shirt or sweatshirt, nylon or pique knit, dark or light garment, etc.?

Most any type of heat press that can provide 40 to 45 pounds of evenly spread pressure can be used for transfer work. It should also be able to maintain the required temperature of 350° to 400°F.

Most of your prospects will know little or nothing about transfers. You can add a name or combine transfers or even add embroidery. Stir up your customer's imagination. Show him what you can do for him. And then, sell . . . sell . . . sell!

CHAPTER 7

BUILD YOUR OWN PRINTER

When I first began screen printing ten years ago, I ordered a 4–color carousel printer with two stations. The manufacturer supplied two platens, one for a child's shirt, one for an adult. I ordered the printer together with a flash cure heating unit. With shipping and packing charges, my total cost came to around $1000. Today, the same equipment setup would come to around $1500.

PLATEN BOARDS

To broaden my service offerings, I looked around and located some scrap formica pieces at a discount lumber yard. I took these reject kitchen counter parts to a local cabinet maker and had him cut platen tops of 10"x10", 14"x14" (shirt platens) and 4"x18" (sleeve platen). The cabinet maker rounded all corners. My total cost for these was $25.00.

Soft pine boards 4"x14"x1" were attached to each platen table. I measured and drilled holes matching the holes on the printer station box. Then 4" bolts with wing nuts were attached so that each platen would provide a quick changeover depending on the job being printed.

Then I took all my platen boards (including those furnished

with the printer) and turned them face down. With 1"x2" boards and 3" screws, I made plates all around each platen so I could easily apply hand clamps. In this way I could use hand clamps to tie down jackets as well as other garments being printed. A 'tie down, is required to keep jackets from moving during the print process.

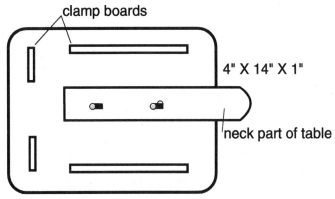

Bottom side of platten showing "tie down" clamp boards

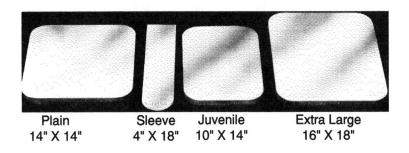

Plain	Sleeve	Juvenile	Extra Large
14" X 14"	4" X 18"	10" X 14"	16" X 18"

Various size plattens

I employ three clamps for T–shirts, five clamps for sweatshirts and all seven clamps for jackets. Jacket tie downs can cost anywhere from $200 to $350 and up. My seven clamps with plastic gloves from the local hardware store cost $25.00. My jackets don't move while being printed.

Whenever multiple colors are required additional screens are required, one screen for each color. It will take time and patience to align each screen color on the press.

MICRO SCREEN ADJUSTMENT ATTACHMENT

Attachments that allow one to micro-adjust each screen are available. If you plan only one color printing, you do not need this screen adjustment attachment. With many multicolor printers, these micro adjustments are built into the printer.

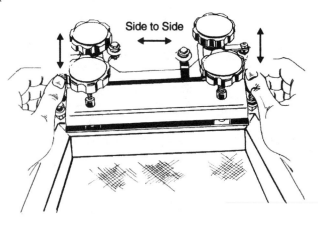

Side to Side

Screen adjustment attachments have been designed to attach to pre-existing equipment and permit operators to move screens on the press in various directions, moving fractions of an inch with each adjustment. Once completed, the screen is locked in place. This process is required until all color screens are locked in.

BUILD YOUR OWN PRINTER

You can make your own printer with a little ingenuity, a couple of 2x4,s, a table to anchor to, and a few parts. And you are in business.

Your discount lumber yard can provide 2x4,s. A cabinet maker can help with a 14"x16" platen. Look for scrap formica pieces that can be trimmed down to size.

Materials List

1 - Long 2"x4"x36" support base to be bolted to table

1 - Long 1"x4"x20" base of platen

1 - 14"x16" formica board for platen

2 - 2"x4"x6" (for either side of support base)

1 - 2"x4"x18" (for support of hinge board)

1 - 1"x4"x18" (for jiffy hinges for screen)

1 pair jiffy hinges

2 - 1/2"x4" nuts, washers, bolts

2 - 3/8"x3" bolts, washers, wing nuts (for platen)

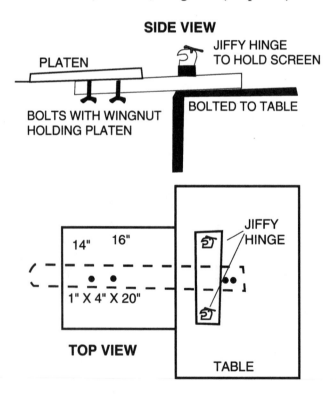

SIDE VIEW

JIFFY HINGE
TO HOLD SCREEN

PLATEN

BOLTED TO TABLE

BOLTS WITH WINGNUT
HOLDING PLATEN

14"   16"

JIFFY
HINGE

1" X 4" X 20"

TOP VIEW

TABLE

BUILD YOUR OWN SCREEN CARRIAGE

or purchase it from your supplier. This unit can be attached to own home built printer.

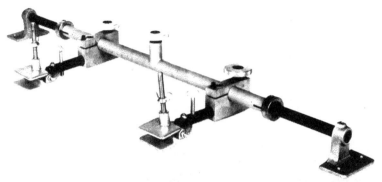

NAZ-DAR/KC REG-STR-RITE SCREEN CARRIAGE

SPECIAL NOTE

Anyone wanting to secure ready made platen (your shirt table with tie-down) may write to the author at address on front page. A youth & adult size will be available at low cost for those unable to secure materials for them. Write for pricing and availability.

Also available through the author is the Livingston Hat Clamp. Write for details.

The Author

CHAPTER 8

THE T–SHIRT

The T–shirt has become a human billboard. It has become the way to flash a message to strangers, friends, or anyone who cares to notice. They are wearable souvenirs for those who travel. They are simply human bumper stickers for those who stay home. They can advertise our loyalty to a company, a product, or some brand name. They tell what school we attend or advertise the city, beach, state, national park, recreational or sporting attraction we visited. For many, the T–shirt is what silk screening is all about.

Before you learn how to load and print your first T–shirt, it is best you learn something about the T–shirt.

Everyone knows that the T–shirt is simply a short-sleeve pullover shirt. If you look it over, you see a body, two short sleeves and a neck. But when you dress it up, it is an entirely new ballgame.

T–SHIRT SIZES AND WEIGHTS

T–shirts come in all kinds of sizes and weights. They are manufactured by many different companies. Hence there are brand names you can identify with and depend upon for quality. T–shirts are available in 100% cotton and blends of cotton and polyester fabrics (including the popular 50/50 blend). The average weight of a large T–shirt is around 5.5 oz. The body length averages around 30", sleeve length 8 3/4", and chest size 22". The shrinkage averages around 5 - 7%. Most T–shirts come in youth sizes XS (2-4), S (6-8 yrs.), M (10-12 yrs.) and L (14-16). Adult sizes are: S (32-34), M (36-38), L (40-42), XL (44-46), XXL (48-50) and up.

When printing both youth and adult shirts, it is well to remember that the average small T–shirt for youth has a body width of about 13". The average adult small shirt has a width of about 17". If you use 8 1/2"x11" transparencies to make your screens, you should only have one screen to make and be able to print on both sizes of T–shirt. If you want to cover more of the adult shirts, you will need to make larger transparencies. Something you need to keep in mind.

There is approximately 1/2 ounce difference in the weight of a 50/50 blend T–shirt and the heavyweight full cut 50/50 shirt. Approximately the same weight difference exists between 50/50 and the 100 full cut heavyweight. It may not seem like much but you will become accustomed to noticing the difference while handling and comparing them with your customer.

FULL CUT

Full cut is supposed to mean bigger than standard,

particularly regarding width. However, it is always well to check this out when purchasing. Make a comparison with your tape measure.

Athletic cut is another measure taken to mean the shirt is bigger than the standard. We all know that athletes tend to be bigger and it follows that the shirts should be both wider and longer as well as have longer sleeves.

SWEATSHIRTS

It is easy to add a note here to include measurements as they pertain to sweatshirts (fleece). Keep in mind that it costs more to add an extra inch here and there to a shirt. A sweatshirt will add even more. Sweatshirts in recent years have become heavier and heavier. The 7.5 ounce used to be common. Then it was 9 ounces. Now it is 11 ounces and going on 12 ounces.

The biggest difference you will find in sweatshirts, other than weight, has to do with the sleeves, both in length and diameter. The sleeve angle on a raglan sleeve can be critical because the angle-cut directly affects the size of the armhole. Other problems could include the neck opening. Can the kid get his head through the opening? How about the wrist band? Can a big hand get through it?

Sweatshirts do not have to be as long as a T–shirt because

they usually are worn outside the pants. But the measurement length always includes the waist band. Just added information to be aware of.

Your customers probably don't know the difference or care, but sweats are put together with side seams (sewn together on each side) or body size (only one seam). Quality should be seen in the sewing: neat and strong. Otherwise, don't worry.

PRINTING AREA

The typical printing area according to size can be seen in the design below. If printing onto the shirt pocket, the heart size is reduced to pocket size of 3" wide (or can cheat to 3 1/2" wide if you are careful). We noted above that it is possible to combine the full size and youth size together into one size.

All printing of T–shirts (or any garment for that matter) begins with cleanliness. That means clean boards, clean

FULL SIZE
10 1/2" WIDE

YOUTH SIZE
8 1/2" WIDE

HEART SIZE
4 1/2" WIDE

SLEEVE SIZE
3 3/4"W X 12" L

press, clean squeegee, and anything else that can contribute to fingerprints or smudges on the work you are doing. Smudged work means loss of income.

You begin with laying out your work. For years, I have used the back of an office chair. I lay out the T–shirt with side to be printed facing me as I pick up each garment. Most often you will be printing the front of the shirt. Of course, many times you will be printing over the pocket area in front with the large imprint on the back. At any rate, layout your shirts based on the order you plan to work. Keep in mind you may be working with sizes (youth and adult - or sizes within each group). Or you may be working colors which means changes in print color. That means cleaning the screen after each color. Make sure to separate all shirts and sizes so you need clean the screen the least number of times. Working in this manner also enables you to keep tab of the numbers of each category in your customer's order.

PLATEN LAYOUT

Before lining up and setting your screen in place, you need to be aware of your platen and how it sets. You will be placing your shirts on the platen so you should know exactly where the center of your platen is in regard to length and width. It will become easy once you have printed for a short time.

Begin by drawing a line (that will show through your shirt) down the middle of the platen (length). Then draw a line where the shirt pocket (4"x4") would normally be in relation to the first line drawn. Shirt pocket is located on your left side. Measure equal distance on right side for another square (4"x4"). This will help determine the area for name. Keep in mind that some customers will want their logo on the left side with name on right. Others will confuse you and want the reverse. Make sure you ask and note it on your layout sheet.

Most T–shirts will have a crease down the center of the shirt. You can line this up with the line you drew down the middle of your platen. This will center your shirt on the platen.

Next you can center and tape your image transparency to

the platen. Now you can line up your screen with the print area on the platen. Platen, shirt, and image on the screen must all line up for a perfect printed shirt.

Of course, proper registration of the image on the screen begins with placing the image transparency on your exposure unit. Then you line up the coated screen with your transparency. Care here will ensure proper registration as you attach your screen to the printing press.

POCKET/NAME AREA

Whenever you are required to print the heart area (pocket) or place a name in a given area, you might consider printing directly onto the platen. Then lift the screen away while you place (and tape) a heavy piece of cardboard (Cut cardboard slightly larger that the imprint.) over the printed image on the platen. Now you can arrange the shirt properly as you feel the card outline under the shirt and know exactly where it is going to print on the shirt.

PRINTING THE SHIRT

Now back to the printing of the shirt. Best to begin with a practice run on newsprint (old newspaper) or old T–shirt. This practice run will ensure your print will be correct. By lining up this practice run it will confirm that proper registration will follow.

Now here we go, with your thumb and forefinger of each

hand, grasp the shirt tail. Spread your hands apart and swing the shirt over the platen, allowing the back of the shirt to fall back under the platen. The front of the shirt is spread over the platen. Align the shirt crease with the line on the platen and adjust the shirt print area over the cardboard on the platen.

If you use hand clamps, clamp one clamp at the neck and one at each side near the center of the platen. These clamps will keep the shirt from moving during printing. Or if you prefer, you can keep the shirt from moving by applying a light spray of adhesive directly on the platen. The spray will last for 20 to 30 shirts before you will need to repeat the spray process.

After printing the shirt you will again use your thumbs and forefingers and pull the shirt off the press, making sure that you keep the shirt from folding together or smudging as you place the shirt onto the dryer (or shirt press) for curing.

PRACTICE RUN

Place an old T-shirt or just a newspaper on the platen for a test run. Lower the screen within an inch or two of the platen. With putty knife or spatula scoop place ink onto the screen near the image area (at the top of screen). Smear ink onto the squeegee as well. Pull the squeegee across the image area toward you, covering the entire image area. This is called the flood stroke. The flood stroke simply gets ink ready to print. Lower the screen into print position. Hold squeegee at 45° angle. Press down on squeegee and pull across the image until entire image is covered. Repeat the flood stroke and raise the screen. Analyze your print. If it looks good, you are ready to print.

You may make mistakes, misprint a few shirts and may not be too happy with your first results. I assure you that repeated efforts will help you develop your skills and in time you will be proud to see your shirts parade around your neighborhood.

Practice your run-through steps several times a day. Mentally anticipate the various things you do and the order in which they are done. You will be surprised how this mental practice will improve your actual steps. Thinking it through will help you act it through — successfully.

CHAPTER 9

CAPS

Caps can become an integral part of your screen printing operation. Caps are the most popular 'giveaway, item for both large and small firms. They can become an easy repeat sale for your business as well. Frequently there will be a combined cap and T–shirt order (e.g., Team sports, marathons, company uniforms, etc.). Caps may be the initial order that begins a long term relationship with a client. T–shirts, sweatshirts, and jackets can come later.

There are many types of caps but initially it is best to restrict yourself to two basic types: the foam-front baseball cap and the golf cap. Of course, there are many other kinds in between.

The most popular cap has been the foam-front baseball cap. For printing purposes it is good to know that this cap comes with a higher crown. The work area can be 3 1/2" high by 5 1/4" wide. However, when laying out the image to be printed on the cap area, you will find it a lot easier to handle if you reduce the area to 2 1/2" to 2 3/4" high by 4 1/2" wide. You can still put an impressive 'billboard, on the cap even at this reduced size.

The artwork for your cap presents an arched top (crown) with a level bottom. The crown in the middle presents the highest part of the arc. Being oval, the design must affect both upper sides of the artwork. The bill of the cap also restricts the boundaries on each side of the bottom.

Several cap layouts are shown here. Note that the four corners of the cap are drawn in so that the image area is necessarily affected at each corner.

GOLF CAP

The golf cap is generally more desirable than the summer-style mesh-back baseball cap. They are a better quality, being all cloth, and therefore command a higher price as well. The golf cap usually has a foldout liner that can be folded out of the way during printing. They also have a smaller crown so that the image area should be restricted to about 2 1/2"x4 1/2". Since the crown is shorter the cap may not fit properly on the cap platen. Some golf caps are stiff and hard to print on. Try to locate a golf cap that has a soft front, is easy to print on and fits your cap platen. Caps that have a soft front with a light buckram backing will print easily and hold shape well. Most cap suppliers are willing to send you samples of their caps for a small fee. They can select a sample display that will help you analyze their catalog.

Restaurants, bars, car dealerships, and many other business firms select the golf cap for their promotional giveaways. They encourage their employees to wear their caps for advertising purposes. The golf cap contributes to their goals of name recognition. Everyone likes to receive things . . . especially a good quality golf cap they would be happy to wear.

PRINTING THE CAP

There is a simple cap attachment that can be clamped to your printer. It sells for under $200.00. The cap bill is held out of the way while the crown front is clamped into position for printing. The crown is held flat so your regular screen can print both the foam-front baseball caps and the all-cloth golf caps.

With a cap heat press you can apply heat transfers onto light color caps. Bear in mind that many transfers will not work on dark materials.

CAP HEAT PRESS

When I create my own cap transfers I add a powdered adhesive onto the wet transfer before the transfer is semi-cured in the oven. I pour a small amount of the powdered adhesive onto a newspaper. Then with the transfer in one hand (and holding the newspaper in the other hand), shove the transfer under the powder, shake off the excessive adhesive back onto the newspaper. I place six to eight transfers onto a rigid piece of cardboard and hold it in the oven (180° - 220°) for six - eight seconds. This achieves a semi-cure and permits working with the transfers without smearing. The heat will bond the adhesive to the plastisol. Then you can center the transfer on the cap and hold in position with heat tape. The heat tape will not leave any marks on the cap and is easily removed with transfer paper. The transfer will require eight to ten seconds at 375°F on the cap heat press to complete the cure. This completes the transfer to the cap.

You will want to order five-panel caps. This means the front is designed for printing. Six-panel caps are tough to deal with because the seam runs down the center of the front of the cap.

Be prepared to screw up a few caps before you begin to get it right. Use the squeegee to print ink onto the cap, not into it. If you push the squeegee too hard, you will smear the design. On the other hand, if you are too timid you won,t get enough ink onto the cap. With a little practice, you will do fine.

Livingston Systems (1-800-624-4381) has engineered a cap clamp that attaches to your printer. It allows you to use any of your screens. The clamp pushes the bill of the cap out of the way and clamps the front of the cap into position for easy printing. They have recently improved on their first model (which I still use). Their newer model provides additional platens that make it easier to handle youth caps and the new lower profile caps.

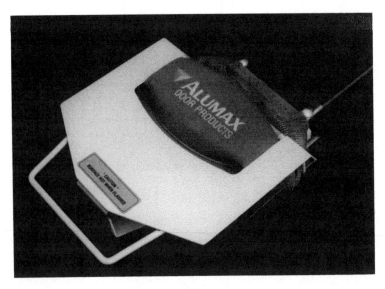

CAP LAYOUT SHEET
To Be Used With ANY Cap Order

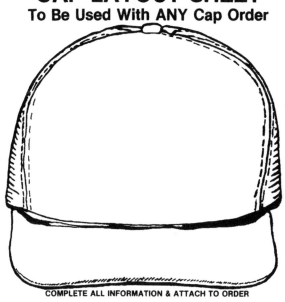

COMPLETE ALL INFORMATION & ATTACH TO ORDER

Line Name _____ ASI # _____

Customer Name _____ Sales Rep Name _____

Quantity Caps_____Style #_____Summer Mesh_____Winter Foam_____

COLORS: Front Panel_____Back_____Visor_____Scrambled Eggs_____

IMPRINT COLOR(S) _____ Flat _____ Puff _____

Comments: _____

_____

ASI# refers to cap catalog, e.g., Staton, Nissin, Otto, etc.

CHAPTER 10

JACKETS

Screenprinters' greatest fear of printing on nylon jackets is related to cost. It is one thing to make a mistake on a $2 T–shirt. But it is really upsetting to ruin a $25 jacket. But jacket printing is not difficult if you have the proper equipment and supplies.

NYLON INK CATALYST

Most all ink suppliers have a direct print nylon silk screen ink. It has the look and printing ease of a plastisol. Most include a two-part catalytic system in which the catalyst has been stirred into the nylon plastisol ink just before use. Be aware that you must mix the catalyst thoroughly. (Note: There is a one-part system on the market, but it needs to be checked out for good adhesion.)

Normally the ratio of regular nylon ink to the catalyst is around 10:1. Do not undercatalyze. If I am mixing just a regular plastisol ink, I add a little additional catalyst to the mix.

The pot life of the mixed catalyzed ink is four to eight hours. But if you should overcatalyze the mix, the pot life is shortened. But when the ink and catalyst are stored separately they have an indefinite shelf life. However the catalyst is extra-sensitive to air and sunlight. It should not be left uncapped or it will harden. When added to the plastisol, it may reduce the viscosity temporarily. If too thin, leave the mix for an hour or so and it will stiffen up for easier printing. However, if too thick, it may be thinned with 3-5% mineral spirits.

The printed jacket must be cured like all plastisols. The average time and temperature cycle is two minutes at 375°F with flash cure unit being six to eight inches above the jacket. The time may vary depending upon the ink deposit, the fabric and type of heat used. A soft sheen will develop when the cure is complete. It will not air dry. Do not launder for 48 hours after printing.

JACKET HOLD-DOWN

It is important that the jacket not move during the printing. Linings of jackets tend to allow the jackets to move. Jacket 'hold-downs, have come to the rescue of screen printers. There are any number of jacket hold-downs. Most are simply a lock-down frame that holds the jacket securely. They can cost anywhere from $200 to over $500.

You can make your own jacket hold-down, as I have. Secure 1"x2"x12" boards on either side underneath the length of the platen. Three-inch screws will do the job. Make sure that tip of screws do not penetrate the top of platen (which will hold shirts being printed). Then add 1"x2"x4" at base of platen. Then purchase seven handgrip clamps from your local hardware store. Make sure that these clamps have rubber or plastic tips so they will not damage jackets.

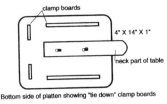

Bottom side of platten showing "tie down" clamp boards

PRINTING THE JACKET

Place the jacket on the platen and pull the jacket tight all around the platen. Use clamps to hold the jacket in place: two clamps on both sides, two at the base and one at collar (top).

Before printing, I use household iron and iron the jacket in the image area. Be sure to use a protective Teflon sheet to protect the jacket. This technique will flatten the pillow effect of the lining — especially quilt lining. Ironing the jacket softens the material and makes it easier to print.

You may use the flash cure unit to dry the nylon jacket. Hold above garment and cure for two minutes. Remember that nylon will scorch at 350°F so monitor your drying cycle.

You may wish to give the jacket only quick cure for eight to ten seconds with your flash cure unit and finish out with shirt press for two minutes (held 1-2" above jacket).

SCREEN MESH 160

I use retensionable as well as wooden frames for printing jackets. Make sure there is good screen tension. Screen mesh can be 160.

To ensure good off-contact printing, you may place a flat thin stick on top of the jacket to hold screen off jacket. The screen should be 1/16" to 1/8" off the jacket. Also, make sure the stick is positioned so that it will not interfere with printing the design on the jacket.

When printing a leftside front design (for name or logo), I place a heavy piece of cardboard to register where it will print. I print the design onto the platen and tape the heavy cardboard over the print. This helps you to print on the right place (near the snaps) as well as line up the jacket before printing.

Use a 70 durometer straight edge squeegee that will leave very little ink on the screen following the squeegee pull.

Try to lay down your print with one pass. You may make a flood stroke to load the ink into the image area on the screen. In this way you will avoid a possible double stroke or miss a spot due to a light touch. For wash-up, use mineral spirits.

Jackets are a high-priced item and popular with consumers and therefore a money maker for the screen printer.

JACKET FABRICS

Every fall and winter there is a wealth of new jacket fabrics offered by printwear distributors. You see antron, oxford, canvas, canton fleece, nylon (Sution is also nylon.), and denim. All these now come in a variety of jacket styles. You may print directly onto poplin as well as denim jackets with regular plastisol inks. No catalysts involved.

JACKET PRICING

Jackets are a popular as well as fashionable item. Jackets make your consumers feel good. They love to wear jackets that promote their school, social club, or place of business. Most jacket printers price their finished jackets by doubling the price of the jacket. One printer estimated that his shop would screw up at least one jacket per order. So make sure you cover the cost of at least one jacket with your pricing. But if you are careful, you can avoid 'screw-ups,.

FLAKING

Should a customer bring back a jacket that has part of the printed area ink flaking after washing, it generally tells you that the jacket was undercured. If it were undercatalyzed, the ink would have peeled off whole, not be flakes.

WATERPROOF or WATER-RESISTANT JACKETS

There is a difference between waterproof and water-resistant nylon jackets. A water-resistant nylon would be slow to absorb water, but would eventually become soaked if water were allowed to remain on the jacket.

Water-proof nylon on the other hand means exactly that. Water will not soak into the jacket. But waterproof jackets usually require some alcohol wiping before printing.

I recommend that you order and stay with domestic (made in U.S.A.) garments. Most foreign-made nylon will often melt before 300°F. This eliminates multicolor designs that demand heat-cure ink system. Most domestic nylons will not start to melt until about 340°F.

JACKET

CHAPTER 11

OFF-CONTACT PRINTING

When correctly set, off-contact distances makes the screen printing process easier. The squeegee causes momentary contact between stencil (screen) and the substrate (garment). The screen rebounds immediately after the squeegee passes over it. This is called 'snap-off,. This is a result of the downward force of the squeegee against the tension of the screen and the off-contact distance.

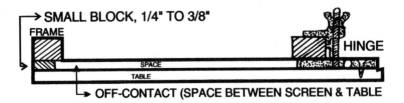

OFF-CONTACT (SPACE BETWEEN SCREEN & TABLE

Low tension screens require more pressure to move the squeegee across the screen. This causes extra friction and resistance between the squeegee blade and the screen mesh.

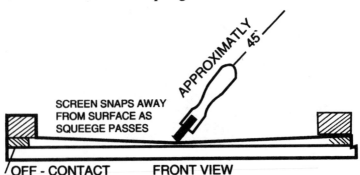

OFF - CONTACT   FRONT VIEW

(Added note - Flat head screws have been used to adjust desired off - contact height)

But with high-tension screen, and a correct off-contact distance (from 1/8" to 1/4") you will witness good snap-off as a result of the squeegee forcing ink through the open areas of the screen.

In contrast, printing on-contact drives ink into the garment. It can also be a source of smearing and smudging on the garment. The key is proper tension as well as being slightly off the garment for proper results. Larger screens with the image located near the center will improve the snap-off.

With heavier screen frames (metal and oversized) the screen has difficulty of keeping off the garment. The screen can be helped by taping small shims under the screen to ensure off-contact printing. You can refer to jacket chapter where a thin smooth stick was placed on the garment to hold the screen 1/16" to 1/8" off the garment. Or use four wood screws if using wood frames.

KICK LEG
This is designed to hold screen off the garment after it has been printed. make your own or order from your supplier.

A small piece of wood screwed or clamped to the side of frame.

You may compensate for loose screen tension by making the distance higher off-contact and add more squeegee pressure. Improper screen tension will cause the screen fabric to roll ahead of the squeegee. This contributes to smeared and blurred prints. Remedy for these problems is solved with correct screen tension.

THE SQUEEGEE

The squeegee brings your screen image, the ink and your garment together. It is probably the only device that is the most crucial but most often it is the least considered and most mistreated around the press.

Someone once wrote that there is no one way to pick the right squeegee for a given job. Then he quickly added that there were five things that should be considered. They were mesh tension, mesh count, ink viscosity, and ink type, The substrate being printed and the desired effect on the printed substrate. He never got around to the squeegee. But we will.

SQUEEGEE SHAPE

Squeegees come in a variety of blade shapes. However, the most commonly used are those with rounded or square edges.

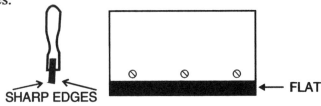

SHARP EDGES   ← FLAT

The shape of the squeegee blade affects both the amount of ink as well as the clarity of the image printed. The square edge is the most common and most accurate. It deposits the smallest amount of ink and leaves sharpest image.

Rounded edge blades improve coverage by allowing extra ink to roll under the blade. The extra angle will deposit more ink onto the substrate.

TYPES OF SQUEEGEES

Rubber squeegees are the least expensive. Although they are low cost and used extensively, you need to know that rubber is susceptible to strong solvents. They also suffer from poor abrasion resistance.

Neoprene is a synthetic rubber material and makes for a popular squeegee. It is only slightly more expensive than rubber but has better chemical and abrasion resistance.

Urethane is another synthetic plastic material used for squeegees. It is more expensive than rubber and neoprene but offers much better resistance to both physical and chemical abrasion.

DUROMETER HARDNESS

Durometer is a measure of the hardness and/or softness of the squeegee blade. It has a numerical value of compression that ranges from 55 to 90. A blade between 55 - 65 is considered soft; 66 to 75 is considered medium; and everything over 75 is considered hard.

It is hard to tell one durometer squeegee from another so most manufacturers have color-coded their synthetic squeegees by durometer. Each manufacturer will furnish proper color charts you can pin to the wall.

There are a number of factors that may affect the squeegee and its ability to perform. Screen abrasion slowly dulls the squeegee. Harsh solvents can often cause the blade to swell. A nicked or dull squeegee will prevent ink to transfer evenly through the screen. You can resharpen squeegee blades with either a belt sander or a high speed grinding wheel. However, you must be careful with the grinding wheel. Too much pressure will tend to melt the edge. Remove as little material as possible over several passes.

Small shops printing Tees and other garments use the standard rectangular squeegee made of synthetic or rubber, and most often they will be in the 55 to 75 durometer range.

Take care of your squeegee. Clean them properly after each use. Make sure ink is cleaned around the cracks where the handle fits the blade. Also avoid leaving them in solvents that tend to soften the blades.

CHAPTER 12

BLANK EMBLEMS / PATCHES

There are several firms that manufacture and supply patches and emblems for special projects. The suppliers listed below have quick turnaround service and their prices are competitive.

Most blanks are made of poly/cotton 65/35 twill fabric with Pelon backing. They are die-cut to shape and then merrowed with a coordinated color rayon yarn border. These blanks are available in many color combinations. They are custom-made according to your needs.

They will also offer both a screen printing and embroidery service. Heat seal backing is available.

Cap or T–shirt heat pressers are required to apply heat seal patches to caps or the printwear garments.

When silk screening on the patch, there is need to build up the print area due to the merrowed border. One needs to ensure that the squeegee applies ink evenly onto the patch area. Practicing a few times will provide a confidence that the job can be serviced properly. It is best to always order a few more patches than required. This allows for some patch printing mistakes. It also provides an inventory cushion should the client require additional patches.

Get into the habit of using the phone and speaking with your suppliers. Don't hesitate to inform them that you are learning and appreciate their understanding and patience with your questions.

Some patch suppliers will silk screen your printing requirement for additional charge. If so, you would only have to apply the patches to your caps/garments. Check out their delivery schedule and inform your client as to schedule time as well.

EMBLEM/PATCH SUPPLIERS

Athletic Sewing Center, Inc.   1-800-531-5406
7210 Eckhert RD
San Antonio TX 78238

EMC   1-800-443-9553
P.O. Box 398
120 Park ST
Rogue River OR 97537

Both companies do custom embroidery.

EMBROIDERY
You will no doubt run into a number of potential clients

who will one day want their shirts or jackets specially embroidered. Embroidery is not like starting screen printing. A typical start-up investment can be $30,000 to $40,000 and that does not count recruiting qualified help to run the operation. In fact, they claim it can take upwards of four to six months to become sufficiently experienced to run the equipment.

CONTRACT EMBROIDERY WORKOUT

Before you begin thinking about embroidery, take the best way into embroidery and contract the work out. Locate someone (business) who does embroidery and check out the cost for subcontract work. Take the time to understand the embroidery industry before considering such a major financial investment.

You may find out that you cannot make any money in this specialized field of embroidery. If so, it would be good to find out early.

Contract embroiderers usually provide the garment and the embroidery. They will negotiate prices, terms, and any other variables for each job. Check them out and go from there.

SPOT CLEANING

Sometimes during the printing process you are bound to get

ink or some smudge on a garment. No matter how it happened, you can clean up the garment and save it from becoming a discard or be forced to reduce the price.

There are several manufacturers of spot cleaning guns. Your regular supplier of equipment can advise you of their recommendation. They are available for around $150 and up depending on size and features.

They are designed to spray a powerful stream of cleaning fluid in a concentrated area to dissolve or break down the ink. You can adjust the nozzle to control the flow from a powerful stream down to a gentle spray.

Remember you are dealing with a chemical so look over the Material Safety Data Sheet (MSDS) from the manufacturer. You should have a separate cleaning area that is well ventilated. Remember Safety First.

You should have a cleaning area where you can place the garment to be cleaned. Then take your cleaning gun and aim it at the ink you wish to remove — holding it about six inches away. The high pressure stream of cleaning fluid should remove the ink and leave the shirt clean and usable. Quick dry the garment to avoid wringing.

Take a little practice to learn how to handle the gun. Test on old rags first. You do not want to blow holes in the shirts you are trying to redeem. Use caution in handling both chemicals and the cleaning gun.

The manufacturers also offer a cleaning station that contributes toward ideal working conditions for cleaning garments and help ensure your safety while handling this equipment.

If you are serious about long term plans, it would be advisable to consider the spot cleaning gun as part of your equipment. Check with your local supplier.

RECLAIMING THE SCREEN

Reclaiming simply means making a used screen mesh act like new again. There is a high cost for keeping screens after every job, hoping to repeat the same job in the future. Keeping used frames can develop into major storage problems as the used screens multiply.

The first step toward reclaiming begins with removing all excess ink from the screen (also the squeegee). Keep in mind that plastisol ink saved by scraping the screen clean can be used and should be replaced in its proper ink container.

Next you need to apply an industrialized strength cleaner solvent to remove all ink and any adhesive residue that remain on the screen. Most small shops simply apply mineral spirits (paint thinner) for this cleaning job.

Recently, I began substituting a strong screen cleaner made from soybean oil. This cleaner is biodegradable. Any waste is drain-safe. The screen is wiped clean with a damp rag.

Once the screen is clean you can begin to work on the emulsion. In my early experience in screen printing, I used to simply wash the screen in bleach water. With government agencies looking over our shoulders at waste disposal practices, you should constantly be looking for solvents that are drain safe and in compliance with governmental requirements.

Consequently, I am currently using a soybean product called 'Strip-E-Doo,. I spray this liquid on both sides of the screen. After two minutes I wash the screen down with the garden hose.

Do not allow this liquid to dry on the screen. This is important. 'Strip-E-Doo, reclaims and degreases in one operation. Rinse and the screen is ready to dry out in a dirt and dust-free drying rack.

If there should still be any haze or ghost images on the screens, there is a de-hazing product (D-Haze) that can clear the screen. Ghost images contribute pin holes and other imperfections on your next use of the screen if not cleared up.

FRANMAR PRODUCTS
BEAN-e-doo™- SCREEN WASH, made from American grown soybeans, removes textile inks, no dangerous fumes.
GREENEWAY™- Screen Wash, a natural organic solvent, removes textile inks.
INKEE DOO 2™- SCREEN WASH, remove plastisol-textile ink from screens without damaging emulsion.

ICKEE STICKEE UNSTUCK[TM] - Adhesive & ink cleaner, removes heavy spray tac & fleece accumulations from platen, also removes ink from screen, squeegees & equipment.

COLOR CHANGE[TM] - On press wash, non aerosol removes plastisol ink from screens for quick on-press clean-ups & color changes.

SOY WAY[TM] - Screen Wash - made from American grown soybeans, removes solvent based inks.

INKEE DOO[TM] - Screen Wash, removes solvent based inks from screens to be reclaimed or stored.

GHOST REMOVER (d-HAZE plus[TM]**)** Removes ink haze, scuz & ghost images & degreases at same time.

EMULSION REMOVER (STRIP-E-DOO[TM]**)** Reclaimer & degreaser, removes all types of emulsion, film, and direct emulsion, fast acting.

RESIDUE CLEANER (Tape-eez[TM]**)** Surface prep & residue cleaner made with corn. Fast evaporating cleaner removes residues associated with screen cleaners.

MESH DEGREASER (D-GREASE[TM]**)** High PH degreasing agent, ready-to-use effective on full range of mesh counts, helps eliminate pinholing, dirt, dust and oils from all types of mesh.

CHAPTER 13

OTHER SUBSTRATES
TOWELS

Towels are used by everyone, every day. Towels can serve as a promotional item or given away as a premium gift.

Towels come in various sizes and weights. The popular beach towel ranges from 30"x60" to 36"x70" and even larger. The bath towel is roughly 22"x44". Your typical hand towel would be 16"x26". A fingertip towel 11"x17". Towels are rated by weight. When a weight is given, it means that would be how 12 such towels would weigh totally. For example, an 11-pound beach towel would be how much 12 of the towels would weigh together.

There are other terry cloth printables, notable bibs and robes. Bibs because everyone loves a baby. Robes because they command a high price tag. But neither of these have the appeal and popularity as the golf and bowling towels.

If you are going in for towels, it means thinking water-based inks. Terry cloth demands enormous amounts of water-based penetration for the fabric to reflect the rich colors you want. Towel printing will also require double-hit squeegee passes with heavy pressure to ensure sufficient ink passes through to the towel.

For screen printing, water-based ink requires water-resistant emulsion. Also, of course, a water-based blockout. Water-resistant tape for taping screens, tape that will not peel under water-based inks.

Oversized towels put demands on your presses as well. It is best you analyze your customer's needs plus changes and/or additions to your regular printing operations. Towels can become a source of added income if you are willing to cover the necessary changes in your operation. Maybe special screen frames to cover the special towel sizes. If you are printing T–shirts, you have the tools to make the transition to towels. The opportunities for success are there.

CYLINDER PRO - Courtesy of Garland Industries

Garland Industries (1-800-621-9549) has come up with a new piece of equipment that can contribute to your service. Their cylinder Pro was new when I saw it at a Printwear Convention a year or so ago. I use it to imprint can coolers. Two firms use can coolers as a giveaway to their employees at the annual company picnic. A fun marathon uses the can coolers as a souvenir at their annual run. One tire company substitutes the can cooler for caps during the summer giveaway program. He can give two coolers for the price of one cap.

LICENSE PLATES

License plates are good promotional items that are comparatively easy to print. It calls for a permanent fast-drying ink that will air-dry within a few minutes. They are available in both aluminum and fiberglass. Aluminum plates are easier to work with and cost about 60 cents each plus shipping. Not all supply houses carry them but Tubelite (1-800-238-5280) carries them. License plates are good for car dealers, school booster clubs, and for businesses who like to see their name out front. You can think of others.

MAGNETIC SIGNS

Magnetic signs that cling to vehicle doors can provide another source of income for the screen printer. Magnetic materials come in rolls (24" wide) or precut by size (standard size 12"x18"). They call for an enamel or vinyl ink for screen printing. It is easy to cut and remains flexible under all conditions. They are designed to withstand continuous exposure to weather and fluctuating temperatures.

REAL ESTATE SIGNS

Real estate firms are good prospects for signs easily screen printed on foam board material. This is a lightweight sandwich of polystyrene foam. 'For Sale, signs are seen everywhere. They must be screened for outside use to withstand weather conditions.

POSTERS

Political signs show up periodically. Special events need a poster announcing the time and place. Contractors want everyone to know where they are working or have done their work. Again a continuing source of business if you wish.

CHAPTER 14

EQUIPMENT
BUYING USED EQUIPMENT

Buying used equipment can be frightening. Equipment can be anything from "barely used, to 'barely usable". You need to check over used equipment very carefully. If you do not know much about equipment, take someone who does along with you. If you are checking out a dryer or anything electrical, be sure you check them out with the power on.

Most used equipment is sold 'as is, and 'where is,. No warranty given. It will be up to you to check it out and move it from the seller's property. It is up to you to determine whether the equipment will meet your needs.

You can look in the advertising sections of the printwear trade magazine (see appendix) and you will find several used equipment dealers. Call several of them and check out their inventories, terms, conditions, shipping, and so on.

As a rule you should expect to pay from 1/2 to 2/3 of the original selling price when buying used equipment. Physical conditions may cause the price to fluctuate up or down. The equipment's age should determine the amount of wear and tear inflicted and directly affect the price. If the owner exercised good regular maintenance, the equipment still may have many years of useful life left when purchased.

NEW EQUIPMENT

There are ten firms listed in the appendix who manufacture and supply new screen printing equipment. Half of those listed have 4-color printers listed for $1000 or less. Each can point out the various advantages of its equipment. Choice of equipment should first be directed toward the screen printer individualized needs. If you are considering new equipment, begin by gathering catalogs and literature that can help your decision making. Why not start with the ten firms listed and give them a call.

The exposure unit is another piece of equipment that will require some attention. If new, it can cost from $1200 to $3000 and up. Again it depends on what whistles and switches are desirable. One unit can double as a light table just by hitting a switch. Another is large enough to process two large screens at a time. Decisions . . . decisions. It begins with you.

With new equipment there are warrantees that follow the equipment from delivery to setup in your shop. There may be follow-up services as part of the deal. Training could also become part of the sale if required. Gather all the information you can. Compare features as well as costs. Ask questions and get answers. Wise decisions can follow.

DRYER

A printwear dryer is not an easy subject. A commercial dryer can cost anywhere from $3000 to $5000 and up. There are so many different types, sizes, energy sources (natural gas, propane, or electric), and of course, different brands. Used equipment can be available from $500 to $1500 and up.

Most dryers come with conveyer belts that are 18" to 48" wide. Because heating chambers come in so many sizes and cover both manual and automatic presses, you will find that dryers can come in many sizes and with lengths from five feet all the way upwards of 60 feet.

There are gas, electrical, or combination models. The physical plant that is available requires major decisions from the start. There are exhaust systems to consider plus all kinds of controls. They are producing smaller units for small manual shops. These are usually 5, to 8, in length. Depending on the work being turned out, some garments may need to be processed through the dryer one or more times.

Building a homemade dryer may be feasible for someone who has the patience, ingenuity, and 'know-how, in both mechanical and electrical areas. This may eliminate most do-it-yourselfers the first time around. A dryer presents these things to think about:

1. Conveyor belt - type of material, conveyor rollers, length and width, belt speed controls
2. Electrical requirements for dryer - what are present limitations - do you need 220 volts, single phase, etc.?
3. Heat chamber length and capacity - future production goals will help dictate choices
4. Safety controls for the heating units - electric (and/or gas-fired units)
5. Adequate insulation to provide safer and more pleasant

working environment.

6. Forced air vs. infrared panels in heating elements - choice again
7. Limitation of space available - always a problem
8. Failure controls to alert operator when electric panel fails or temperature drops below minimum require ments.
9. Exhaust system to remove fumes from system
10. Sheet metal framework

Home-made dryers have been made by individuals and small firms. Costs have been estimated to save $1000 to $2000 depending on the dryer limitation or its size.

FLASH CURE HEATING UNIT

A simple flash curing unit for the small shop is an infrared heating unit. A picture of the 16"x16", 110 volt, 15 amps, 1800 watts unit that I purchased nearly 10 years ago is shown here.

I have had to rewire the cord several times but the unit is still in use today. The unit cost slightly less than $400 and should be available for near the same cost today. It is being used to semi-cure the plastisol print on jackets. Giving the jacket a semi-cure on the press allows for easier handling. It is also used when multicolor printing requires wet on wet printing of shirts. This protects against possible smears.

SHIRT HEAT PRESS (See Chapter 6)

You can use your shirt press for a dryer. After all, you can apply transfers to shirts. I have used my shirt press as a curing unit to dry shirts, fleecewear as well as jackets. I set the heat switch to 375°F and bring the unit to within two to three inches of the garment. Place transfer sheet on top of the wet plastisol print and covered with Teflon. Cure takes approximately 20 seconds. I then place press on the Teflon three to four seconds to smooth the garment and complete the cure. For nylon jackets, keep the press around six or seven inches above the jacket and set the timer for two minutes. Do not allow the press to touch the jacket. You may wish to review the earlier section "Printing the Jacket." Keep a watchful eye during the final 20 seconds of the cure.

CHAPTER 15

NUMBERING SYSTEM

If you are going to do team sports, you will be required to print player's names and numbers on T-shirts, athletic jerseys, and other sporting garments. There are several silk screening systems on the market for around $400.

I have used Sports ID screen printing system for the past two years. They offer precision vinyl stencils. The numbering system includes a stencil for each number from 00 to 99. They can be ordered in your choice of 10", 8", 6", 4", or 3" full block style. Each vinyl number is perfectly spaced, durable and reusable.

The name system has letters in 1", 2", 3", and 4" vinyl letters and accessories. You can build a series of names at a time. There are tracks that hold letters as you build each name. The letters interlock at the top of each stencil and overlap to prevent ink seepage during printing. Once the name is completed, place a strip of masking tape across the top of the stencils to hold each letter in place. I then add a second tape across the bottom before removing the names from the plastic track.

Prepare all names required for the job. Then match names with shirt sizes. You will line up player's name at top of shirt (back side) and print. You will be using blank screen the size of largest name. Begin with shortest name and work up to largest. Once printed, remove player's name and place in container with mineral spirits. When all names have been printed, rinse the stencils with water and dry. After drying return to letter box for reuse.

Each number is a single vinyl stencil placed on the shirt beneath the player's name. Your customer will often ask you to give certain numbers to given players. If so, you will need to reserve the number with the name and, of course, make sure it is placed with correct size shirt. You will love working the little leagues!

Although I have used this system for several years, there are other systems that are worthy of your consideration. Their name and addresses are listed in the appendix section.

J.J.'S FRAMES
MIAMI

FRAME TECH
OF ORLANDO

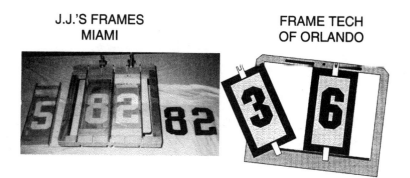

USING TRANSFERS

Many sporting goods dealers and screen printers subcontract their numbering jobs out. Some of these subcontractors apply their athletic names and numbers by heat transfer. Check out Stahl, Dalco, and M&M Designs. You will find their phone numbers and addresses in the appendix.

You do not have to cook the transfers into the garment. Seven to eight seconds using light pressure is most often adequate. First arrange the garment on the press, preheat it to release any moisture and close the press briefly to smooth out garment. Then arrange your numbers, cover with Teflon sheet, press, remove the sheet and you are ready to fold your garment. That's it!

If you plan to do little leagues, here are a few things to remember:

1. Use 2" lettering for player names.
2. Babe Ruth League prefers 3" lettering.
3. Switch to 2" lettering for longer names.
4. Sleeve numbers, if required, can use 3" or 4".
5. Sponsor names should be in 2" lettering.
6. Double check numbers and especially letters before imprinting to make sure not wrong side up or backwards.

7. Double check spelling and layout.

8. 6" and 8" numbers are standard.

LICENSE TO PRINT

If a customer approaches you with a sizable order for reproducing artwork (say, from a book, reproduction of famous painting) and you fear the rights of ownership belong to someone else, what should you do? Since there has been much publicity over National Football League licensing of logos as well as licensing many Disney characters, you had best consider a couple of steps before producing the order.

1. First the customer needs to produce a letter for you which states he has the right to reproduce whatever the artwork he is furnishing.

2. Second, the customer should also provide you with a letter of protecting you against indemnification should you be sued by a third party claiming to be the rightful owner of the artwork. This would protect you against ` any costs you might face in such a suit, including legal fees.

Sports, both locally and nationally, are fast-growing businesses in the licensing fields. Those who hold license for the local sporting field you are interested in may appear reluctant to deal. Start with local retailers first. This could also include the campus bookstore.

To give you an idea as to the magnitude of financial burden you will face, consider the National Football League properties. First, you will have to submit what you have in mind. If acceptable, there follows a minimum guarantee of $10,000 due upon signing the contract. The royalty rate is 9% of wholesale price. This would be a two-year contract. You would further have to have product insurance of $3 million for bodily injury and $1 million for property damage.

Not all licensing operations will demand such costs beforehand. However, it does point up that there are many financial and legal details that attend to securing a license to reproduce copyrighted material.

Most licensing will cover some or all of the following: the product, sale territory, length of term, advance up front, royalty rate, and perhaps a guarantee. If everything is agreed to, you sign agreement, you get the logo or whatever and then you go to work.

There is seldom any problem with the local schools which are glad to furnish layouts of school logos, team mascots, and whatever is required to help them raise funds. But at the higher levels, just be aware that reproducing someone's copyrighted material should raise the caution flag before you plan and do the job presented.

CHAPTER 16

EPA and OSHA

The Environmental Protection Agency (EPA) and the Occupational Safety and Health Administration (OSHA) are two government agencies concerned with the screen printing workshop. The EPA is concerned with the pollution to our environment and OSHA is concerned with the health protection of employees in the workplace.

Each distributor of screen printing suppliers is now required to furnish vital information concerning each of the screen printing products that may pertain to hazardous concerns to employee exposure and waste disposal. Small shops should become aware of whatever regulations are being put in place by both state and federal agencies. You are not allowed to just pour everything down the drain anymore. A one-man shop or a family-run business may not be visited by a governmental agency in the beginning, but one should be concerned about one's health as well as one's employees (as you grow). Become aware of what is required and get in step of caring for your environment as well as community.

SCREEN PRINTER'S RESPONSIBILITY

First, you should evaluate all waste generated to determine if it is hazardous. If not, find out what rules (if any) your state has on the disposal of non-hazardous waste.

You can reduce any future problems by adjusting and focusing on waste from the beginning. In a small shop, this pertains to screen reclaiming chemicals and clean up process. Of course, total volume of waste must also be weighed.

Be aware that petroleum-based products like mineral spirits and lacquer thinner are two products often used by the new screen printer. Ghost images that show up on the screen are often removed by using a caustic acid solution. Some solvents leave a grease or oil residue that call for a degreaser.

But now there are new gentler chemicals available to the screen printer. These will make your shop safer and gentler to your health as well.

Most plastisols do not contain any hazardous chemicals and so are drain safe. It is the cleanup chemicals that need to be analyzed and evaluated as to waste. Be informed that there are natural cleansers that allow you to let waste to flow into the sewer system with both local and state approval.

MATERIAL SAFETY DATA SHEETS
Material Safety Data Sheets (MSDS) are reports supplied

by your distributor or manufacturer whenever you order chemicals from your supplier. Although these MSDS reports seem too technical and difficult to read, you should scan them and pick up information that will help you be aware of any hazardous substances contained in the product. The MSDS report also contain any spill cleanup instructions should a spill occur. You need to know if there are any fire or explosion hazards. If there should be health hazards present, you would need to know what appropriate first aid should be given in case of accident. Finally, the report will also contain your responsibilities as to management and disposal.

CHAPTER 17

PROSPECTING FOR BUSINESS

Your business is everywhere but it begins with a customer. Where do they come from? Well, there are family reunions, birthday parties, Grand Openings, Father's Day, Mother's Day, county fairs, restaurant aprons, the racing team, Little League Baseball, football, soccer, volleyball, basketball, special sales, annual golf tournaments, fund raisers, company uniforms, the tire people, businesses of all kinds — yes, they are everywhere.

With business card and flyer, just get out and meet people. Everywhere you go, give them a card, let them know who you are and ask what can you do for them? Do they sponsor an athletic team? Bowling team? Present special awards (jacket, T-shirt) to their employees? How about a family reunion?

Then, there are child care centers. Maybe a special T-shirt as a security aid for field trips or staff uniforms for employees?

The bowling alley is a good place to stop. Get permission to place your card and flyer on the bulletin board.

Who handles the details of organizing little league and adult league athletic programs? Look at the sport page announcements and you will find phone numbers telling you who to call. Call them and let them know who you are and what you can offer.

Go to the laundromats and tack your card and flyer on the bulletin board. Do this every so often because someone always takes them down every so often.

Rodeos. Show up and pass your card and flyer around.

Every marathon needs T-shirts.. Look to the calendar of events in the sports section. Find the organizer and get in touch.

Whenever you see a grand opening, follow up with your card and flyer. You might be too late for the opening but the business is ongoing and could use your help.

Get in the habit as you see new buildings being constructed. There are many contractors who need caps, T-shirts, jackets and business cards to promote their business. Leave your card and flyer as often as you can.

Company picnics are a once-a-year deal. If you can, search

them out. Then, these can generate additional business from those attending.

Every fund-raiser needs T-shirts to let the helpers advertise the event. It also becomes a source of pride for those participating.

Just walking down the street with business card and price flyer in hand, take the time to enter each business and introduce yourself. Seek out the secretary or first one to approach you say something like this, "I am John Paul and I do custom silk screening. Who should I see to make an appointment to describe our services?" Usually you will be told who to see and whether that person is in, available, or should be contacted later for an appointment. Get into the habit of writing the person's name, phone number, and best time to call back.

You may find that you have made 10 to 20 calls this way. You may even have the opportunity to speak with several potential clients about your services on your first visit. Expect this. After all, you have a service that most of these prospective clients need or use. This is one of the best ways to advertise. When I first started, I was nervous, but I was totally surprised when I also got sales. If I see ten people, I expect to sell one. You can do the same. It may take a little time to get used to, but sales will come if you are patient. Learn what you are doing and persist.

My wife told me later, she didn't think I could do it. Now I can tell you, if I could do it, anybody can do it.

PRICING

First remember that you cannot be a small-business person and stay in business without a profit. If you are paying your customers for the privilege of silk screening for them, you will not be in this business very long.

There is no set rule-of-thumb that can tell a small business owner how to set his prices. One thing you don't do is to see what your competitor is quoting and set your prices accordingly. Rather, you need to be compensated for your talents and your investment. Your cost figures, your style of operation, a profit, and a return on your investment should all be considered in your pricing. It will be rather difficult to get a good handle on these items in the beginning.

A 100% markup is not out-of-line. That would mean a $3.00 T-shirt should go for $6.00. That is not far from where I start my T-shirts.. Satin jackets costing $20.00 would be considered a $40.00 jacket. Working for free just doesn't pay!

Focus on what you do well, try to improve on what you can. And don't feel as though price makes the deal.

SALES TAX PERMIT

Each state will have its own forms, regulations, and procedures to follow. A telephone call to the state capital can lead you to the proper office to contact and the phone number to use to initiate the necessary steps to follow.

Most of the wholesale supply houses will demand a tax permit before they will process any orders with you. Or they may deal and add the sales tax even though you may be entitled to a tax-free account. So it is important that you contact your state department for a tax permit as soon as possible. Of course, you will not owe any sales tax before you actually sell. However, you may be required to submit a monthly report of no sales for any month that you were actually opened for business even though no sales were being reported for a particular month.

Study the booklet of information that they will send. Then there is an application to be filled out. In time, you will get the permit you need. Then there follows the regular monthly tax reports you will be making. These may stretch out to quarterly reports depending on business being reported.

Make a folder for your tax permit data. You will be required to search out information when required and you will need a place to file information when required as well as a place to file information when received.

BUSINESS CARD

The first form you have should be your business card. Give yourself a name. You want to leave an impression that they will call you later, when they need your services. You do not want them to discard your card. A business card is primarily an easy way to remember your name, phone number, and what you do. You only have five to seven lines of print, so you must make these lines work for you.

You will be in silk screening and at the same time you are in advertising. You may be making political signs or making T-shirts promoting an annual marathon. I started promoting advertising specialties. So I began with a calling card: simply Paul's Advertising Specialties. I have since just dropped the Specialties to make the name shorter. At any rate, Paul's Advertising works for me.

BROCHURE

Again, I started selling advertising specialities. So it was convenient to list many items that most businesses could use to promote their business. But on the second side I was able to advertise the many silk screening items that also caught their attention. Since everyone would want the best prices, it was worth while to quote minimums in my flyer. Most of my business had to do with sport teams (10-15 caps and shirts), business uniforms (Sportshirts, T-shirts, and caps). Again small quantities.

APPOINTMENT BOOK AND DAILY CALENDAR

My appointment book is critical. It tells me where I have been and who I saw: my sales efforts for the day. It records my daily mileage, critical for income tax expense. Also, I note postage paid, miscellaneous items purchased, and the like. Keep a daily diary.

INSURANCE

Insurance is not meant to protect you from every little thing but from a major loss. Keep in mind that operating a small screen-printing shop or home-based business should make you want to check out adequate insurance coverage. If you are a home owner, check to see if a rider could be added to your home owner policy to cover the few additional items for your business. Current value of your equipment less depreciation should be covered. How about computer equipment coverage if you have one plus the software? Keep up-to-date on what it would cost you should any of your equipment need be replaced due to fire, water damage, theft, or some other natural disaster. It is all part of the expense of being in business.

Your insurance needs are something you should talk to your insurance agent about. He could better advise you about what you should cover and in what manner. If you are renting or purchasing equipment, it is necessary that they be protected against possible loss. Look into deductible plans that may increase your coverage and at the same time reduce your regular premium.

Remember that inadequate insurance coverage may kill more business than the natural disasters themselves. Do not allow hindsight to substitute for foresight in insurance matters.

I have used a quotation form to freely quote on T-shirts or caps, etc. I can sketch the art work as well. They may not make an immediate decision but it stays on their desk for a time while they consider whether they can afford the work now. Sometimes it may be six months later that they call to check if the price is still the same. You never know. I make sure to do my part and then wait. Of course, there are follow-ups as well.

BUSINESS RECORDS

I started with a simple check register bookkeeping plan. I keep tabs of all my receipts and check deposits in a box on my desk. I pay everything by credit card or by company check so I have a handle on most all my expenses and income. Then once a month I list all receipts and show a breakdown as to cost of materials, shipping, COD charges, advertising, insurance, customers, amount paid, taxes assessed, etc. Each month is summarized and sales tax computed, expenses noted, and everything ready for both quarterly and end of year totals. Keep it simple, accurate, and current and you can make it work.

APPENDIX

SUPPLIES FOR THE BEGINNER

From your local hardware store:
Masking tape (to tape front and back of screen to prevent ink form leaking onto garment.)
Gallon of paint thinner (to clean screens, squeegees after printing)
Staple gun (for applying screen fabric to frames) Add a box of staples.
Putty knife (use for placing ink from container to screen)
Paint scraper (useful to scrape ink from screen after printing)
Household bleach can be added to water to remove emulsion from screen. (Note: I started out using bleach water but now use soybean wash instead.)

From your supply dealer:
Quart of direct emulsion (emulsion plus additive to be mixed)
Quart of white plastisol ink
Quart of black plastisol ink
Quart of heavy blockout (to cover pin holes and other imperfections in the screen before printing)
One to two yards of 110 mesh fabric to make your screens
One 12-inch medium squeegee
One 8-inch medium squeegee
One 4-inch medium squeegee (for caps)
Small supply (50 to 100 sheets) of transfer paper (for making transfers - also drying T–shirts on shirt heat press)
Spray can of adhesive (to hold transfer paper in place during printing) also can be used to hold garments in place while printing
Quart of powdered adhesive (used in assisting in

transferring a transfer to the cap)

You can add to this list once you begin to screen print your own work. How about some old rags to clean up your messes? Perhaps some discarded T–shirts or other garments to practice on?

THE FOLLOWING FIRMS ARE SUPPLIERS OF SCREEN PRINTING EQUIPMENT.

Check them out. Call for their catalogs. Check with their sales departments and do not be afraid to seek out their advice.

ANTEC (Charlotteville, VA) 1-800-552-6832

CATCO (Coral Springs, FL) 1-305-752-3369

HIX (Pittsburg, KS) 1-800-835-0606

HOPKINS (Alameda, CA) 1-800-233-8333

IRISH GRAPHICS PRODUCTS (Grants Pass, OR) 1-800-247-3977

NATIONAL SCREEN PRINTING EQUIPMENT (Pittsburg, KS) 1-800-843-3928

ODYSSEY SCREEN PRINTING EQUIP. (Slippery Rock, PA) 1-800-557-7889

RICHARDSON INDUSTRIES (Grove City, OH) 1-800-635-7695

R. JENNINGS (Glen Falls, NY) 1-518-798-2277

STAHL (St. Clair, MI) 1-800-521-9702

PRINTWEAR WHOLESALE DISTRIBUTORS - CALL THESE SUPPLIERS FOR T–SHIRTS, FLEECEWEAR, SPORTSHIRTS, JACKETS, AND MORE.

BODEK & RHODES - (Philadelphia, PA) 1-800-523-2721

BRODER BROS. - (Dallas, TX) 1-800-521-0850

FULL LINE - (Houston, TX) 1-800-385-5463

MID-AMERICA WHOLESALE - (Kansas City, MO) 1-800-366-1416

ONE STOP - (Grand Rapids, MI) 1-800-968-7550

STATION WHOLESALE - (Dallas, TX) 1-800-888-8888

WESTARK GARMENT MFG. - (Ft. Smith, AR) 1-800-783-9007

ATHLETIC WEAR (SPORTING GOODS)

EMPIRE SPORTING GOODS - (New York) 1-800-221-3455

NEW SOUTH - (North Carolina) 1-800-438-9934

FOREMOST ATHLETIC - (Texas) 1-800-272-8700

REDA - (Pennsylvania) 1-800-444-REDA

BOMARK - (Texas) 1-800-231-3351

THE FOLLOWING FIRMS ARE SUPPLY DISTRIBUTORS. They can furnish inks, emulsions, mesh fabrics, frames, screens, art supplies, reclaiming chemicals, and much, much more. Some of them also represent manufacturers of screen printing equipment.

DIAMOND CHASE (Frames) (California) 1-714-891-3234

FRANMAR CHEMICAL (Normal, IL) 1-800-538-5069

FRAME FAST (St. Paul, MN) 1-800-323-4545

GARLAND INDUSTRIES (Cylinder Press) (Texas) 1-800-621-9549

GRAPHIC SUPPLY (Tulsa, OH) 1-800-234-0765

IRISH GRAPHIC PRODUCTS (Grants Pass, OR) 1-800-247-3977

LIVINGSTON SYSTEMS (Hat Champ) 1-800-624-4381

NEWMAN ROLLER FRAME (Pennsylvania) 1-800-523-3694

SERICOL (Kansas City, KS) 1-800-255-4562

TUBELITE (Memphis, TN) 1-800-238-6592

CRYSTAL CORPORATION (The Frame) (Nevada) 1-702-883-8191
CAP SUPPLIERS (The following deal exclusively with caps)

ATT GROUP (Houston, TX) 1-800-939-8866

NISSIN CAPS (Dallas, TX) 1-800-647-7467

OTTO CAPS (Arlington, TX) 1-800-398-6886

OUTDOOR CAPS (Bentonville, AR) 1-800-826-6047

TOWELS (Some of the above wholesale distributors also handle towels.)

MC ARTHUR TOWELS (Maryland) 1-800-356-9168

TOWEL SPECIALTIES (Maryland) 1-800-878-6935

MANUFACTURERS OF PRINTWEAR GARMENTS. They will furnish a complete list of their distributors. You will also learn more about their garments plus they offer sales ideas, highlight new trends, and up-to-date catalogs.

FRUIT OF THE LOOM 1-502-781-6400

HANES 1-800-685-7557

LEE 1-800-680-4440

OUTER BANKS 1-800-438-2029

JERZEES 1-800-321-1138

DICKIES INDUSTRIAL WEAR 1-800-336-7201

AUBURN SPORTSWEAR (Jackets only) 1-800-221-9685

ATHLETIC NUMBERING
AND/OR LETTERING SYSTEMS

SPORTS ID (Michigan) 1-800-435-4384

FRAME TECH OF ORLANDO (Florida) 1-800-699-1550

DALCO (Texas) 1-800-288-3252

STAHL (Michigan) 1-800-521-9702

M & M DESIGNS (Texas) 1-800-627-0656

DYCO (Kansas) 1-800-835-0340

SOURCE LIST OF SOME TRANSFER
MANUFACTURERS

AIR WAVES (Ohio) 1-800-468-7335

C T M MFG (Florida) 1-800-233-3454

DALCO ATHLETIC (Texas) 1-800-288-3252

JOY INSIGNIA (Florida) 1-800-526-7148

PRO WORLD (New Jersey) 1-800-678-8289

STAHL'S TRANSFER (Ohio) 1-800-622-2280

TELETREND (Ohio) 1-800-552-8000

CLIP ART

Dynamic Graphics, Inc., 6000 N. Forest Park Dr., Peoria, IL 61656-1901; (800)255-8800

Graphic Products Corp., Wheeling, IL 60090

Valdez Clip Art, Westbury, Long Island, NY 11590

Volk Clip Art, P.O. Box 347, Washington, IL 61571-0347; (309)685-8055

Some clip art providers have their clip art on CD ROM.

Image Works (800)900-4077

Creative Software Solutions (800)910-9955

Small Designs (800)959-7627

SOURCE OF LEADING MAGAZINES:

iMPRESSIONS - P.O. Box 41529,
Nashville, TN 37294-9927
PRINTWEAR -   P.O. Box 1416
Broomfield, CO 80038-9922

THE PRESS -   P.O. Box 12986
Overland Park, KS 66282-9708

GLOSSARY OF REGULARLY USED TERMS BY SCREEN PRINTERS

ABRADE - To roughen up a mesh surface to allow emulsion to adhere better to the fabric.

ACETONE - A volatile, flammable liquid that is often used by screen printers in removing water coatings from image areas to be printed on nylon jackets.

ADDITIVE - Anything added to a substance or formula to alter its functioning. For example, adding a retardant to a water-based ink to slow drying in the screen.

ADHESIVE - A special spray or liquid used to temporarily hold a garment or paper to a platen (pallet) during printing.

AIR DRIED EMULSIONS - Emulsions that have dried by air temperature in a dark room.

APPLIQUE - A decoration cut from one fabric and stitched to another to add dimension and texture. Often used as a substitute for embroidery.

ART WORK - The original design laid out for making a screen.

BASE - A specific class of resins that determines the character of the ink by the ink manufacturer such as acrylic base, oil base, vinyl base, synthetic base, etc. Or it may refer to an extender base that is a modifying additive for screen printing inks such as transparent base.

BIODEGRADABLE - The ability of a substance to decompose and breakdown into smaller compounds. Often used in contrast to hazardous waste.

BLEEDING - The moving of ink or pigment into an unwanted area (e.g., one ink mixing with another and forming a third color that becomes a 'discolor, on a print.

BLEND - Describes the fabric content (e.g., a 50/50 blend of cotton/polyester).

BLISTER - Air bubbles that get trapped between capillary film and the screen.

BLOCKOUT - A heavy liquid that dries rather quickly into a film to prevent ink from passing through a screen. Used to fill pin holes, fish eyes, and the like found in the screen before printing.

BONDING AGENT - An additive that gives ink a better adhesion to such substrates like nylon (see catalyst).

BRIDGING - Crossing fabric threads at the edge of a stencil (e.g., stapling screen to a frame).

BUCKRAM - A coarse woven fabric stiffened with glue and used in caps to hold front panel erect.

BUTT-TO-BUTT - A registration technique where one color is placed up against another color on a printed surface. The edges of each color meet exactly without overlapping.

CAMERA-READY-ART - Everything in the print design is set in correct size, proper place, and all lettering finished as it is to appear in final reproduction.

CAPILLARY FILM - Stencil film adhered to a wet screen via capillary action, filling the fabric mesh openings. This is done before exposing the screen.

CHENILLE - A form of embroidery in which a loop stitch is formed on the top side of a fabric.

CLIP ART - Camera-ready art that is not copyrighted and can be purchased from clip art service or is free.

CATALYST - A substance that has capabilities to speed the reaction between two (or more) substances. E.g., an additive to nylon ink before imprinting nylon jacket.

CLOGGING - Blocking of mesh opening by some foreign matter that prevents the complete design from being printed.

COAT - To put emulsion onto a screen.

COLD-PEEL TRANSFER - A design printed on paper with plastisol ink applied to a garment by heat. However, the paper is removed only after it has cooled. (See Hot-Peel Transfer.)

COLOR SEPARATION - Separation of a multicolor design into its primary colors. Then individual screens for each color are prepared and applied to recreate full-color design.

CONTACT PRINTING - The process in which the entire screen mesh is in contact with the surface of the garment being printed. (See off-contact printing.)

CONTRACT PRINTING - Screen printing firms print specific jobs for another company. Most often the company will supply the garments as well as the camera-ready artwork.

CONVEYOR DRYER - A dryer that incorporates a conveyor belt that moves garments through a heating chamber.

CURING - A process by which plastisol inks are fused (cured) with temperature between 280°-375°F.

DEFINITION - The quality of the edge of the stencil. Sharp as opposed to fuzzy.

DEGREASER - A compound used to remove grease, dirt and other chemicals left behind by oil-based inks. To be removed before emulsion is applied to a screen.

DEHAZE - The process of removing 'ghost, images that may be left behind in a reclaimed screen.

DEPOSIT - The ink design as printed on the substrate. (That is a garment or whatever is being printed.)

DIRECT EMULSION - A stenciling process by coating a liquid photosensitive chemical onto a screen and exposed with a transparency (photographic positive film). The unexposed emulsion is then washed from the screen and the stencil is then dried and made ready for printing.

DUROMETER - An instrument used to determine the hardness of rubber in a squeegee.

EMBLEM - Commonly an insignia of identification.

EMBROIDERY - Decorative stitching on fabric.

EMULSION - A liquid photosensitive coating for the screen.

EXTENDER - A chemical (or modifier) added to the ink to increase its volume without decreasing viscosity (fluidity).

FABRIC - Material stretched over the frame which supports the stencil. Also called mesh and comes in various weaves from coarse to fine.

FILM POSITIVE - A positive image made of photographic film. Picture of artwork, preparatory to making screen. Also called a transparency.

FISH EYES - Small, thin spots that show up in the surface of emulsion after drying. Usually resulting from dust particles or oil spots that prevent the emulsion from adhering properly to the screen.

FLASH CURE - A partial curing (fusing) process of plastisol inks, most often used in multicolor printing between color applications.

FLOOD STROKE - A non-print stroke to prime the screen before the print stroke. It can also be made to keep the area moist between prints.

FOUR-COLOR PROCESS PRINTING - The process of producing a full-color design from the original artwork.

FRAME - A square or rectangular shaped form, made of wood or metal, to which a screen fabric is attached.

FULL ATHLETIC CUT - This refers to garments that have been cut to fit an athletic build that usually means slightly oversized from normal sizing. This normally refers to measurements that include upper chest, armhole, body width, and sleeve opening.

GHOSTING - An image of the printed design that remains on the stencil even after the screen has been stripped and washed.

HAND - The feel of ink on the substrate,s (garment) surface. A 'soft, hand has a light touch or feel. 'Heavy, hand would be like puff ink or the heavy feel of raised letters on athletic jerseys.

HEAT TAPE - Tape that is not affected by heat and is used to hold transfers in place while applying heat and pressure of the press.

HEAT TRANSFER - The process of transferring a design from a specially treated paper onto a garment (or cap) using a temperature of around 375°F.

HOLD DOWN - A device attached to the press to 'hold down, nylon and other lined jackets firmly to the printing pallet to prevent any movement during the printing process.

HOT PEEL TRANSFER - A type of transfer printed with a special plastisol formulation peeled from the backing sheet while still hot (as opposed to being cooled first).

I.D. - Abbreviation for 'inner dimension, for a second screen measurement.

IMPRINTING - This is the result of transferring an image by pressure.

LIGHT TABLE - A table with lights built-in under a

glass top used for tracing, making overlays, cutting screen film, and spotting negatives.

LINE ART - Art that is all black and white with no tones or colors.

LOGO - This is a name, symbol, or trademark of a company, school, or organization.

MASKING - The process of blocking out the areas on the screen, which will not print.

METAL-HALIDE LAMP - A non-harmful light source often used to expose screen stencils.

METALLIC INK - Powdered metals such as aluminum, bronze, and other metals processed with ink to give appearance of gold, silver, or some other color.

MONOFILAMENT - Silk screening fabric woven with single strand material.

MONOGRAM - A design composed of one or more letters such as initials in a name. Most often relate to embroidery.

MULTIFILAMENT - Silk screening fabric made of two or more strands of material twisted around each other.

NEWTON - A unit of measurement indicating the relative tension of a stretched screen (usually expressed as N/CM or Newtons per centimeter).

O.D. - Abbreviation for 'outer dimension, used for a screen frame measurement.

OFF-CONTACT PRINTING - A silk screening

technique where the screen is positioned above, rather than on, the surface to be printed, touching the substrate only at the point of squeegee contact.

OPACITY - The ability of an ink to keep light from penetrating. (E.g., completely hiding the color of the garment where covered by the ink).

OSHA - Occupational Safety and Health Administration of the U.S. Department of Labor. They cover health standards concerning handling hazardous substances in the work place.

OXIDIZING - The ability of an ink to air-dry. Many water-based inks can be dried in this way. Plastisol inks must be dried by applying heat.

PALLET - The surface that supports a garment during the printing process. Also called the shirtboard or platen.

PIGMENT - An additive that creates the apparent color in an ink.

PIN HOLES - Small undesirable holes on photo screen due to dust on the screens. Need to be blocked out before printing.

PLASTICIZER - A non-evaporative oily chemical used to add flexibility to plastisol printing inks.

PLASTISOL - A family of inks containing a plasticizer used by screen printers.

PLATEN - Another name for pallet (or shirtboard).

POLYESTER - Any manufactured fiber. Polyester

fibers are known for their ability to resist wrinkles.

POSITIVE - Transparency or film copy of artwork to be reproduced onto screen.

POT LIFE - The amount of time that a material may maintain usefulness. For example the normal storage life for inks or other materials when kept under recommended conditions.

PRIMARY COLORS - For printing inks, they are yellow, magenta, and cyan. For light, they would be red, green and blue.

PUFF INK - An ink that expands when heated and thus gives off a three-dimensional look.

RECLAIM - The process of cleaning stencils and inks from screens in order to reuse these screens.

RETARDER - A liquid added to slow the drying time of ink.

ROPE AND GROOVE - A method of stretching mesh fabric onto a frame. The mesh is driven into a deep groove that runs around the backside of the frame. A cord or rope is pushed into the groove by a special hand tool.

SCOOP COATER - A tool used to coat the screen fabric with emulsion.

SCRAPER - Also a tool that can be used to coat a screen. Likewise, can be used to remove excess ink from a screen.

SCREEN - Mesh material stretched over a frame with

stencil attached, ready for printing.

SHOULDER-TO-SHOULDER TAPING - This refers to shirt or garment. Usually a half-inch strip of fabric running from one shoulder-edge, across the back of the neck and on to the other shoulder-edge to reinforce critical stress points of the seams of the shoulders.

SLACK - A term to denote loose screen mesh.

SOLVENT - A liquid cleaner used in dissolving or thinning silk screening inks.

SPAI - A professional organization for silk screeners. An abbreviation for Screen Printing Association International.

SQUEEGEE - This is a rubber or plastic blade usually attached to a wooden handle. It is used to move ink across the screen fabric, forcing the ink onto the substrate being printed.

STENCIL - The part of a screen fabric that creates the printed image.

STRETCHING -Screen fabric being applied to a frame. It applies to the desired tightness or tension of the screen across the open area of the frame.

SUBSTRATE - Any material being printed on. It can be a sign, a poster, or the T–shirt you are printing.

SUBLIMATION - Type of transfer in which dyes are used to transfer a design onto a substrate under heat and pressure. The dyes vaporize and are absorbed by the polyester fibers. This process can be used to print textiles as well as mugs, plates, or other specialty items.

TEMPERATURE TAPES - Specially treated paper used to note the proper temperature of the dryer. They change color at specific temperatures.

TENSION METER - A device used to gauge the tautness of a screen.

TEXTILES - Any fabric that make up garments to be printed.

TRANSFER - The process of transferring a design from a specially treated paper onto a garment by heat and pressure.

TURNAROUND - The time it takes to do a job from the initial job order to the delivery of that job to the customer.

TWO-NEEDLE HEMMING - Designates the degree of fluidity of a compound (flow of ink). Low viscosity indicates thin and high viscosity is thick.

VACUUM FRAME - Part of the screen printer,s exposure unit that is used to hold down the positive tightly against the screen during exposure. This can also be achieved by placing a window glass with a weight attached to ensure holding positive against the screen.

WATER-BASED INK - Inks that have a water base as opposed to a plastisol (oil-based).

WET-ON-WET - Printing one color over another color before the first color has been dried.

TROUBLE SHOOTING DIRECT EMULSION

PROBLEM SOLUTION	POSSIBLE
Poor definition	Check positives against screen Wash from both sides Improve coating technique Use finer mesh
Stencil softness	Check procedure Review storage guidelines Use new positives Dehumidify work area
Open area haze	Use new positives Check screen Use safelights; store coated screens in dark Check washout procedure
Emulsion washing or peeling during washout	Upgrade fabric stretching and coating procedures Review coating procedures Check procedure Degrease all fabric; roughen and degrease synthetics Washout below 100`F Review storage guidelines Build drying box Increase exposure;

dehumidify   shop

**Pinholes/fisheyes appear
before exposure**

Degrease
Housecleaning overdue
Cover coater and
          emulsion
Slow down; turn screen
180` after each stroke
Allow 1-hour (min) for
de- bubbling

**Pinholes appear after

exposure and washout**

Dry in dust -
free

environment
Wipe positives; Use
     window cleaner on
     contact glass

Pinholes on press

Upgrade coating method
Use solvent-resistant
     emulsion
Alter wash-up technique
Assuming proper coating
and exposure, use abrasion
resistant emulsion

**Details remain closed after
wash-up**

Use fresh emulsion for
     fine details
Work under safelights;
     store coated screens
     in dark
Dry below 100`F
Check density
Use finer mesh; use faster
     exposing emulsion;
     upgrade light source

Wash very thoroughly
from both sides
where possible, min
exposure distance
should be 1 1/2
times image area
diagonal

SCREEN PRINTING

PROBLEM	POSSIBLE SOLUTION
Smeared copy	Add more ink and remix. Use a firm, clean fill pass; do not allow ink to drip onto the screen from the squeegee blade Set off-contact so that only the area under the squeegee blade contacts the surface; the screen should lift clearly from the surface directly behind the squeegee. Tighten hinges Remake screen; fabric
colors	must be taut and uniform
Mis-registry on multiple	Tighten hinges Use a direct emulsion stencil. Block out most of well area before applying stencil. Air dry only between colors on tight register work. Make squeegee pass in one direction on all colors.